THE SOUL OF A WOMAN

THE
SOUL OF
A
WOMAN

ON IMPATIENT
LOVE, LONG LIFE,
AND GOOD WITCHES

Isabel Allende

Cover design by Elena Giavaldi
Cover image: © Charlotte Johnstone / Bridgeman Images

The Library of Congress has established a
Cataloging-in-Publication record for this title.

ISBN: 978-0-593-40143-9

www.penguinrandomhouse.com/large-print-format-books

FIRST LARGE PRINT EDITION

Printed in the United States of America

10   9   8   7   6   5   4   3   2   1

This Large Print edition published in accord with
the standards of the N.A.V.H.

TO PAULA, LORI, MANA,
NICOLE, AND THE OTHER
EXTRAORDINARY WOMEN
IN MY LIFE

THE SOUL OF A WOMAN

WHEN I SAY THAT I WAS A FEMINIST in kindergarten, even before the concept was known in my family, I am not exaggerating. I was born in 1942, so we are talking remote antiquity. I believe that the situation of my mother, Panchita, triggered my rebellion against male authority. Her husband abandoned her in Peru with two toddlers in diapers and a newborn baby. Panchita was forced to return to her parents' home in Chile, where I spent the first years of my childhood.

My grandparents' house in Santiago, in the Providencia neighborhood, then a residential district and now a labyrinth of offices and shops, was large and ugly, a monstrosity of cement with high ceilings, drafts, walls darkened by kerosene-heater soot, heavy red plush curtains,

Spanish furniture made to last a century, horrendous portraits of dead relatives, and piles of dusty books. The front of the house was stately. Someone had tried to give the living room, the library, and the dining room an elegant varnish, but they were seldom used. The rest of the house was the messy kingdom of my grandmother, the children (my brothers and me), the maids, and two or three dogs of no discernible breed. There was also a family of semi-wild cats that reproduced uncontrollably behind the refrigerator; the cook would drown the kittens in a pail on the patio.

All joy and light disappeared from the house after my grandmother's premature death. I remember my childhood as a time of fear and darkness. What did I fear? That my mother would die and we would be sent to an orphanage, that I would be kidnapped by pirates, that the Devil would appear in the mirrors . . .

well, you get the idea. I am grateful to that unhappy childhood because it provided ample material for my writing. I don't know how novelists with happy childhoods in normal homes manage.

Early on, I realized that my mother was at a disadvantage compared to the men in her family. She had married against her parents' wishes and the relationship had failed, just as she had been warned it would. She'd had to annul her marriage, which was the only way out in that country, as divorce was not legalized until 2004. Panchita was not trained to work, she had no money or freedom, and she was the target of gossip; not only was she separated from her husband, but she was also young, beautiful, and coquettish.

———

MY ANGER AGAINST MACHISMO STARTED in those childhood years of seeing my mother and the housemaids as victims.

They were subordinate and had no resources or voice—my mother because she had challenged convention and the maids because they were poor. Of course, back then I didn't understand any of this; I was only able to do so in my fifties after spending some time in therapy. However, even if I couldn't reason, my feelings of frustration were so powerful that they marked me forever; I became obsessed with justice and developed a visceral reaction to male chauvinism. This resentment was an aberration in my family, which considered itself intellectual and modern but according to today's standards was frankly Paleolithic.

Panchita consulted several doctors trying to find out what was wrong with me; maybe her daughter suffered from colic or a tapeworm? An obstinate and defiant character was accepted in my brothers as an essential condition of masculinity, but in me it could only be pathological. Isn't it always thus? Girls are denied the right to be angry and to thrash about. We had some psychologists in Chile, maybe even child psychologists, but in a time dominated by taboos, they were the last resource for the incurably mad. In my family, our lunatics were endured in private. My mother begged me to be more discreet. "I don't know where you got those ideas. You will acquire a reputation of being butch," she told me once, without explaining what that word meant.

She had good reason to worry about me. I was expelled from school—run by German Catholic nuns—at age six, accused of insubordination; it was a prelude to my future. Maybe the real reason I was expelled was that Panchita was a single mother with three kids. That should not have shocked the nuns, because many children in Chile were born out of wedlock, but not usually in our social class.

For decades I considered my mother a victim, but I have learned that the definition of victim is someone who has no control or power over her or his circumstances. I don't think that was her case. It's true that in my early childhood my mother seemed trapped, vulnerable, and sometimes desperate, but her situation changed later, when she met my stepfather and started traveling. She could have fought for more independence and the life she wanted; she could have developed her great potential instead of submitting. But I know that's easy for me to say because I belong to the feminist generation. I had opportunities that she didn't have.

———

ANOTHER THING I LEARNED IN MY FIFTIES in therapy is that the lack of a father in my childhood likely contributed to my rebelliousness. It took me a long time to accept Uncle Ramón—as I always called the man Panchita paired up with when I was about eleven years old—and to understand that I couldn't have had a better father.

I realized this when my daughter, Paula, was born; he fell madly in love with her (it was mutual), and for the first time I saw the tender, sentimental, and playful side of the stepfather against whom I had declared war in my adolescence. I had hated him and questioned his authority, but he was an invincible optimist and never even noticed. According to him, I was always an exemplary daughter! Uncle Ramón had such a poor memory for anything negative that in his old age he called me Angelica, my middle name, and said I should sleep on my side so as not to crush my wings. He repeated this up until the end of his life, when dementia and the fatigue of living reduced him to a shadow of the man he had once been.

In time, Uncle Ramón became my best friend and confidant. He was cheerful, bossy, proud, and a male chauvinist, although he denied the last, arguing that no one was more respectful to women than he. I was never able to fully explain to him how his tremendous machismo manifested. He left his wife, with whom he had four kids, and his wife never consented to an annulment of the marriage, which would have allowed him to legalize his relationship with my mother. That didn't stop them from living together for almost seventy years. At the beginning, there was scandal and gossip, but later on very few objected to their union. Customs relaxed and, in the absence of divorce, couples got together and separated without bureaucracy.

Panchita resented her partner's defects as much as she loved and admired his good qualities. She assumed the role of a dominated and often furious wife because she felt incapable of bringing up her children alone. To be maintained and protected came with an inevitable cost.

———

I NEVER MISSED MY BIOLOGICAL FATHER or had any curiosity to meet him. His condition for consenting to the annulment of his marriage to Panchita was that he would never have to take care of his children, and he took that to the extreme of never seeing us again. The few times his name was mentioned in the family—a subject that was carefully avoided—my mother would get a terrible migraine. I was told only that he was very intelligent and had loved me dearly. I've also been told he would play classical music for me and show me art books, and that at two I could identify the artists. He would say "Monet" or "Renoir" and I would flip through the pages to find the right illustration. I doubt it. I wouldn't be able to do that now, even with the full use of my faculties. In any case, all that is said to have happened before I was three, so I don't remember, but my father's sudden disappearance probably scarred me. How could I trust men who love you one day and vanish the next?

My father's abandonment of us is not exceptional. Women are the pillar of the family and community in Chile, especially among the working class, where fathers come and go and often disappear for good, never to see their children again. Mothers, on the other hand, are trees with firm roots. They take care of their children and, if necessary, others. Women are so strong and organized, it has been said that Chile is a matriarchy.

Even the worst cavemen repeat this fallacy. The truth is that men control political and economic power—they make the laws and apply them at their convenience—and in case that does not suffice, the Catholic Church, with its customary patriarchal zeal, intervenes to support them. Women are the bosses only in their families . . . and then only sometimes.

———

FEMINISM OFTEN SOUNDS SCARY BECAUSE it seems too radical or is interpreted as hatred of men. Before continuing I must clarify this for some of my readers. Let's start with the term **patriarchy.**

My definition of patriarchy may differ a bit from Wikipedia or Webster's Dictionary. Originally it meant the absolute supremacy of men over women, over other species, and over nature, but the feminist movement has undermined that absolute power in some aspects, although in others it persists as it has for thousands of years. Although many discriminatory laws have been changed, the patriarchy continues to be the prevalent system for political, economic, cultural, and religious oppression. It grants dominion and privileges to the male gender. Aside from misogyny—contempt for women—this system includes diverse forms of exclusion and aggression: racism, homophobia, classism, xenophobia, and intolerance of different ideas and people. Patriarchy is imposed with aggression; it demands obedience and punishes those who defy it.

And what is my definition of feminism? It is not what we have between our legs but what we have between our ears. It's a philosophical posture and an uprising against male authority. It's a way of understanding human relations and a way to see the world. It's a commitment to justice and a struggle for the emancipation of women, the LGBTQIA+ community, anyone oppressed by the system, including some men, and all others who want to join. Welcome! The greater our number the better.

In my youth I fought for equality. I wanted to participate in the men's game. But in my mature years I've come to realize that the game is a folly; it is destroying the planet and the moral fiber of humanity. Feminism is not about replicating the disaster. It's about mending it. As a result, of course, it confronts powerful reactionary forces like fundamentalism, fascism, tradition, and many others. It's depressing to see that among the opposition forces are so many women who fear change and cannot imagine a different future.

The patriarchy is stony. Feminism,

like the ocean, is fluid, powerful, deep, and encompasses the infinite complexity of life; it moves in waves, currents, tides, and sometimes in storms. Like the ocean, feminism never stays quiet.

———

No, quiet you are not prettier
You are gorgeous when
    you struggle
when you fight for what is yours
when you don't shut up
and your words bite,
when you open your mouth
and everything around
    catches fire.
No, quiet you are not
    more beautiful,
only a little more dead.
One thing I know about you
and it's that I have never
    seen anybody

ever
so eager to live
shouting

—"BURN" BY MIGUEL GANE

—

I ASSUMED IN MY CHILDHOOD THAT I would have to take care of my mother and support myself as soon as possible. This was reinforced by my grandfather's message. Although he was the unquestionable patriarch of the family, he understood the disadvantages of being a woman and wanted to give me the tools I needed so I would never have to depend on anyone. I spent my first eight years under his tutelage. Later, at sixteen, I moved back in with him when Uncle Ramón sent my brothers and me back to Chile. We had been living in Lebanon, where Uncle Ramón was consul, when in 1958 a political and religious crisis threatened to plunge the country into civil war. My brothers went to a military academy in Santiago and I went to my grandfather's house.

My grandfather Agustín started working at fourteen when his father's death left the family in a helpless condition. For him, life was about discipline, effort, and responsibility. He held his head high: Honor came first. I grew up under the influence of his stoic school of thought: Avoid all ostentation and squandering, don't complain, endure, perform, don't ask for or expect anything, fend for yourself, and help and serve others without boasting.

He told me the following story many times. There was a man who had an only son, whom he loved with all his soul. When the child turned twelve the father told him to jump from the second-floor balcony without fear, because he would catch him below. The son obeyed, but at the last moment the father crossed his arms and let the child crash to the ground. He broke several bones in the fall. The moral of this cruel fable was to trust nobody, not even a father.

In spite of his severity, my grandfather was beloved for his generosity and his unconditional service to others. I adored him. I remember his white mane, his loud laughter, his yellow teeth, his hands twisted by arthritis, his mischievous sense of humor, and the irrefutable fact that I was his favorite grandchild. Undoubtedly he would have preferred another grandson, but in time he learned to love me in spite of my gender because I reminded him of his late wife, my grandmother Isabel, with whom I share a name and an expression around the eyes.

———

IN MY ADOLESCENCE IT WAS OBVIOUS that I didn't fit in anywhere, and it was my poor grandfather's fate to deal with me. I was not lazy or insolent; quite the opposite. I was a good student and I obeyed the rules of coexistence without protest. But I lived in a state of contained fury that didn't manifest in tantrums or door slamming, only eternal, accusing silence. I was a knot of complexes. I felt ugly, impotent, invisible, that I was a prisoner of a boring existence, and very lonely. I didn't belong in a group. I felt different and excluded. I fought solitude by reading voraciously and writing daily to my mother, who by then had moved with Uncle Ramón from Lebanon to Turkey. She also wrote me often and we didn't mind that the letters would take weeks to reach us. That's how the correspondence we maintained for the remainder of her lifetime began.

I have been clearly aware of injustices in the world since I was a kid. I remember that in my childhood the maids at home worked from dawn to dusk, had very little free time, earned a pittance, and slept in cells without windows and with no more furniture than a cot and a rickety chest of drawers. (That was in the 1940s and 1950s. Of course, this is not the case anymore in Chile.) As a teenager my concern with justice only increased. While other girls worried about their appearance and how to attract boys, I was preaching socialism and feminism. No wonder I had no friends. Inequality infuriated me. In Chile, matters of social class, opportunity, and income were appalling.

The worst discrimination was against the poor—it always is—but inequality against women concerned me more. We were light-years from the advances of the feminist movements of Europe and the United States, although we had always had visionary women who fought for better education and participated in politics, public health, science, and the arts. No one in my environment spoke about the situation of women, not in my home, not at school, and not in the press, so I don't know how I acquired that awareness.

———

ALLOW ME A BRIEF DIGRESSION REGARDING inequality. Until 2019 Chile was considered an oasis in Latin America, a prosperous and stable country on a continent shaken by political uncertainty and violence. On October 18 of that year, the country and the world were surprised by an explosion of populist anger. Optimistic economic figures had been released that didn't reflect the distribution of resources or the fact that income inequality in Chile is among the highest in the world. The economic model of extreme neoliberalism imposed by General Pinochet's dictatorship in the 1970s and 1980s privatized almost everything, even basic services like water, and gave carte blanche to capitalists while the labor force was harshly repressed. That created an economic boom for a while, and allowed for the unbridled enrichment of the few, while the rest of the population survived on credit. It was true that according to statistics, poverty had diminished to less than 10 percent, but that figure didn't show the hidden poverty of the lower middle class, blue-collar workers, and retirees. Discontent had been accumulating for more than thirty years.

In the months following October 2019, millions of people marched in the streets of the main cities of the country. In the beginning, the protests were peaceful, but soon acts of vandalism occurred. The police reacted with a brutality that had not been seen since the time of the dictatorship.

This movement, which had no visible leaders and was not linked to any political party, was joined by different sectors of society with their own grievances: indigenous people, students, unions, and professionals. And, of course, feminist groups.

———

"YOU ARE GOING TO BE ON THE RECEIVING end of a lot of male aggression and will pay a high price for your ideas," my worried mother warned me. With my character I was never going to get married, and spinsterhood was the worst fate. One became a spinster around twenty-five years old, so speed in landing a husband was necessary. Girls took great pains to catch a boyfriend and get married quickly, before other, smarter girls got the best matches. "I also abhor machismo, Isabel, but there's nothing to be done; the world is like this and always has been," Panchita told me. I was a voracious reader and what I had learned in books confirmed that the world changes constantly and humanity evolves, but the changes are only obtained after much struggle.

I am impatient; now I understand that I was trying to inject feminism into my mother against her will, without considering that she was from another era. I belong to the transitional generation—between our mothers and our daughters and granddaughters—that imagined and propelled the most important revolution of the twentieth century. It could be argued that the Russian Revolution of 1917 was the most remarkable, but the feminist revolution has been deeper and more lasting: It affects half of all humankind. It has spread and touched millions and millions of people and offers the strongest hope that this civilization in which we live could be replaced by a more evolved one. That both fascinated and scared my mother. She had been brought up with another of my grandfather Agustín's axioms: **Better the devil you know than the devil you don't.**

Maybe I have given you the impression that my mother was one of those formal matrons typical of her social class and generation. Not at all. Panchita didn't fit the usual mold of ladies of her time. She feared for me not because she was prudish or old-fashioned but because she loved me very much and because of her personal experience. I am sure that without knowing it, she planted in me the seeds of rebellion. The difference between us was that she could not have the life she would have preferred—in the country, surrounded by animals, painting, and walking in nature. Instead she submitted to her husband's wishes. He decided their diplomatic destinations, sometimes without consulting her, and imposed his preference for an urban and gregarious lifestyle. They had a very long but conflicted love affair because, among other reasons, the demands of his career went against her own inclinations. I, on the other hand, was independent from a young age.

Panchita was born twenty years before I was and missed riding the feminist wave. She understood the concept and I think she wanted it for herself, at least in theory, but it demanded too much effort. She thought it was a dangerous utopia that in the end would destroy me. Forty years later she realized that far from destroying me, it had forged me and allowed me to do almost everything

I had wished for. Through me, Panchita could make some of her dreams come true. Many of us daughters have had to live the lives that our mothers could not.

———

DURING ONE OF OUR CONVERSATIONS IN our later years, after much struggle, some failures, and a few victories, I told Panchita that I had been subject to a lot of aggression, as she had predicted, but that for each blow I received I delivered two. I could not have lived in any other way, because my childhood anger only grew over time. I never accepted the limited feminine role imposed upon me by my family, society, culture, and religion. At fifteen I walked away from the church forever, not for lack of faith—that came later—but because of the inherent machismo of all religious organizations. I cannot belong to an institution that considers me a second-class member whose authorities, always male, enjoy complete impunity and enforce their rules with dogma.

I defined myself as a woman on my own terms, blindly. Nothing was clear. I had no models to emulate until later, when I started working as a journalist. Mine were not rational or conscious decisions; I was guided by an irresistible impulse. "The price I have paid for half a century of feminism is a real bargain, Mom; I would pay it again multiplied by a thousand," I assured her.

The moment came when it was no longer possible to hide my ideas from my grandfather, but then I got a surprise. That old man, proud of his Basque origin, Catholic, antiquated, stubborn, and wonderful, was a true gentleman, the kind who pulls out chairs and opens doors for the ladies. He was shocked

by his unhinged granddaughter's theo-
ries, but at least he was willing to listen,
as long as she didn't raise her voice. (A
señorita has to have good manners and
decorum.) That was more than I could
have hoped for and more than I ever obtained from Uncle Ramón, who was a
generation younger than my grandfather
Agustín. He had not the least interest in
a girl's obsessions, let alone in feminism.

———

UNCLE RAMÓN'S WORLD WAS PERFECT.
He was well situated on the upper bar
of the chicken coop. He had no reason
to question the rules. He had been educated by Jesuits and nothing gave him as
much pleasure as a good discussion. To
argue, refute, convince, and win . . . How
delicious! He discussed all sorts of things
with me, from Job's vicissitudes (the Job
of the Bible, tested by both God and the

Devil, was a fool according to him and a holy man to me) to Napoleon (whom he admired and I detested). At the end of each discussion, he always left me feeling humiliated because there was no way I could defeat him at the intellectual fencing he had learned from the Jesuits. The subject of machismo bored him, so we didn't talk about it.

Once, in Lebanon, I told Uncle Ramón about Shamila, a girl from Pakistan who attended my school. She cried because she had to go back to her family during her vacation. Our British school had Protestant, Catholic, Maronite, Jewish, and some Muslim girls, like Shamila. She told me her mother had died and her father sent her to boarding school, far from her country, because she was his only daughter and he feared she would be "ruined." A slip from her would stain the family honor, a stain that could only be washed away with blood. Shamila's virginity was more valuable than her life.

When she returned home, watched closely by a chaperone, her father, a very traditional man, was horrified by the Western customs his daughter had acquired at school. A pure and decent girl had to cover herself. She couldn't look a man in the eye, go out alone anywhere, listen to music, read, or communicate with someone of the opposite sex. She belonged to her father. But fourteen-year-old Shamila dared to question her father's decision to marry her off to a man thirty years her senior, a merchant she had never met. She was beaten and locked up for the two months of her vacation. The beatings continued until her will was broken.

My friend returned to school—thin, mute, and with purple circles under her eyes—to receive her diploma and gather her things. She was a shadow of the girl she had been. I went to Uncle Ramón, thinking that Shamila could escape her fate by requesting asylum from the Chilean consulate. "By no means! Imagine the international problems that could result if I am accused of whisking a minor away from her family. That's the equivalent of kidnapping. I am sorry about your friend, but you can't help her. Be grateful that that's not your reality," he told me, and proceeded to convince me to embrace a less ambitious cause than trying to change centuries of Pakistan's prevailing culture.

By the way, forced child marriage is still practiced in countries like Yemen, Pakistan, India, and Afghanistan, and in parts of Africa, usually in rural areas. But it also takes place in Europe among immigrants, and in the United States among certain religious groups. It has dramatic physical and psychological consequences for girls. The photojournalist and activist

Stephanie Sinclair has dedicated much of her life to documenting child brides with her photos of girls forced to marry men as old as their fathers or grandfathers, and of girls who are impregnated in puberty, before their bodies are ready for pregnancy and motherhood. (You can see her work at stephaniesinclair.com.)

———

FOR MY GRANDFATHER, A COUPLE'S RE-lationship was simple: The man provides, protects, and orders; the woman serves, cares for, and obeys. For that reason, he believed marriage is very convenient for men but a bad deal for women. This was advanced thinking for his time. Now it's been proven that the happiest people are married men and single women. The day he led his daughter, Panchita, to the altar, he told her for the umpteenth time not to marry, that there was still time to turn around, leave her fiancé standing there, and politely dismiss the guests. He repeated the very same thing to me at my wedding a couple of decades later.

In spite of his radical opinions about marriage, my **tata** Agustín was very traditional regarding femininity. Who determines what tradition and culture enforce? Men, of course, and women accept it without questioning. According to my grandfather, one had to be a **señora**—a lady—in all circumstances. It's not worth the time to expand on the meaning of **señora** for my family; it's too complicated. Suffice to say that the sublime example would be the impassive and distinguished Queen Elizabeth II of England. In the 1960s she was young, but even then she behaved impeccably, as she has continued to do throughout her long life. At least that's what she shows in public. For the old man, it was not appropriate for any woman, let alone a woman of my age, to express her opinions, which possibly were of no interest to anybody. Mine regarding feminism fell into that category.

Somehow I managed to have him read **The Second Sex,** by Simone de Beauvoir, and some articles that I left lying around his house, which he pretended to ignore but sneakily leafed through. My proselytizing made him nervous, but he endured my barrage of facts—how women suffer disproportionately the impact of poverty, lack of healthcare and education, human trafficking, war, natural disasters, and violation of their human rights. "Where did you hear that?" he would ask suspiciously. Frankly, I don't know, because my sources were scarce. Google wouldn't be invented for another forty years.

"Don't make **Tata** and Ramón

angry, Isabel," my mother begged me. "Everything can be handled elegantly and without noise." But there's no feminism without noise, as we would ascertain later.

—

MY FIRST JOB, AT SEVENTEEN, WAS AS A secretary copying forest statistics. With my first paycheck I bought pearl earrings for my mother and then started saving for marriage, because despite my mother's concerns I had somehow managed to trap a boyfriend. Miguel studied engineering and was tall, shy, and sort of a foreigner, because his mother was English, his grandfather German. He had been in a British boarding school since age seven, where caning was the preferred method of teaching the United Kingdom's Victorian virtues (which were of little value in Chile).

I clung to him desperately because I am romantic, I was in love, and in a blatant contradiction of my feminist preachings, I feared spinsterhood. I was twenty years old when we got married. My mother sighed, greatly relieved, and my grandfather warned the groom that unless he could tame me, like a horse, he was going to have a lot of problems. He asked me sarcastically if I indeed intended to observe the vows of fidelity, respect, and obedience to Miguel until "death do us part."

Miguel and I had two children, Paula and Nicolás. I made a great effort to fulfill my role as wife and mother. I didn't want to admit that I was dying of boredom; my brain was turning into noodle soup. I imposed on myself a thousand tasks and I was running around like a poisoned mouse trying to avoid confronting my fate. I loved my husband and I remember the first years with my young kids as a very happy time, although inside I carried a burning restlessness.

—

EVERYTHING CHANGED FOR ME IN 1967 when I started working as a journalist at **Paula,** a newly launched feminist magazine. (The name has nothing to do with my daughter's; it was one of those names that suddenly became popular and omnipresent.) The editor was Delia Vergara, a young and beautiful journalist who had lived in Europe and had a clear vision of the type of magazine she wanted. With that in mind, she gathered her small team. The magazine saved me from being suffocated by frustration.

We were four young women in our twenties ready to shake up Chilean prudery. In our country, which was very conservative and had a provincial mentality, social mores had not changed much over the last century. We got inspiration from magazines and books from Europe and North America. We read Sylvia Plath and Betty Friedan, and later Germaine Greer, Kate Millet, and other writers who helped us define ideas and express them eloquently.

I opted for humor because I soon realized that the most daring ideas can be accepted if they elicit a smile. That's how my column "Civilize Your Troglodyte" came to be. It made fun of machismo, and ironically became very popular among men. "I have a friend who is just like your troglodyte," they would say to me. (Always a friend.) Some female readers, on the other hand, felt threatened because the column shook the very foundation of their domestic world.

I was comfortable in my skin for the first time. I wasn't a lonely lunatic; millions of women shared my concerns. There was a women's liberation movement happening on the other side of the

Andes Mountains and our magazine intended to spread it throughout Chile.

From those foreign intellectuals whose books we read, I learned that anger without purpose is useless and even harmful; I had to act if I wanted change. **Paula** magazine gave me the opportunity to transform into action the awful restlessness that had tormented me since childhood. I could write! There were hundreds of taboos directly related to women that we wanted to challenge in our pages: sex, money, discriminatory laws, drugs, virginity, menopause, contraception, alcoholism, abortion, prostitution, jealousy, just to name a few. We questioned sacred notions like motherhood that demanded the sacrifice and total self-denial of one member of the family. We aired secrets like domestic violence and even female infidelity, which was never mentioned; it was a male privilege, although a simple mathematical calculation sufficed to prove that women were as unfaithful as men. Otherwise, who were men sleeping with? It couldn't always be with the same small group of volunteers.

My three colleagues and I wrote with a knife between our teeth; we were a scary gang. What did we want to change? Nothing short of the whole world. With the arrogance of youth, we thought that could be done in ten or fifteen years. This was more than half a century ago and look where we are still today. But I have not lost faith that it can be achieved, and my accomplices from that time, who are as old as I, haven't either. And yes, I use the word **old,** which seems to be pejorative. I do so on purpose because I am proud of my age. Every year I have lived and every wrinkle I have tell my story.

———

THE POET AND ACTIVIST SYLVIA PLATH said that her greatest tragedy was to have been born a woman. In my case that has been a blessing. I had the chance to participate in the women's revolution, which is changing civilization as it consolidates, albeit at a crab's slow pace. The more I live, the happier I am with my gender, particularly because it enabled me to give birth to Paula and Nicolás. That transcendent experience, which men still can't have, defined my existence. The most joyful moments of my life were holding my newborn babies to my breast. And the most painful moment was holding my dying daughter in my arms.

I didn't always like being a woman; as a girl I wanted to be male because it was obvious that my brothers had a more interesting future than I did. But my hormones betrayed me. Around the age of twelve I got a waist and a couple of plums appeared on my chest. Then I started thinking that even if I couldn't be a man, I was going to live as one. I achieved it with tenacity, effort, and luck.

Rationally, few women could be as satisfied with their feminine condition as I because they endure infinite injustice as if that were a divine curse, but as it happens, despite everything, most of us like being women. The alternative seems worse. Fortunately, the number of women able to overcome the limitations imposed on them is growing. A clear vision, passionate heart, and heroic will are required to master the fatigue and defeats of the journey. That's what we are trying to instill in our daughters and granddaughters.

———

I ASKED SEVERAL FEMALE FRIENDS AND acquaintances if they were happy with their gender and why. It's a tricky question because we have come to understand the concept of gender is fluid, but for simplicity's sake I will use the terms **woman** and **man.** Though this was admittedly an unscientific and small sampling, the responses were incredibly interesting.

The women said they liked being female because we have more empathy and solidarity than men and we are more resilient. As we give birth, we bet on life, not on extermination. We are the only possible salvation for the other half of humanity. Our mission is to nurture; destruction is masculine.

Someone refuted this affirmation, arguing that there are women as bad as the worst men. True, but the greatest predators are men. Ninety percent of violent crimes are committed by men. In every circumstance, in war as in peace, within the family or at work, men impose themselves by force; they bear the most responsibility for this culture of greed and violence in which we live.

One woman in her forties referenced

testosterone, which generates impulses of aggression, competition, and supremacy. She told us that her gynecologist prescribed her that hormone in a cream, to be rubbed on the belly to increase her libido. She had to stop because she grew a beard and drove her car with an intention of running over the first pedestrian who crossed her path. She concluded that it's preferable to live with less libido than to shave and live furious.

They also said there's a certain looseness in being female. Men are trained to repress emotions; they are limited by the straitjacket of masculinity.

One of the participants in my mini poll said that men have mothers who could have brought them up to be more gentle. I reminded her that only modern feminists can try to forge our sons' mentality. Historically, mothers have not been able to oppose the patriarchy. Even today, in the twenty-first century, a submissive, isolated, uneducated woman, a victim of the male chauvinist tradition, which goes back millennia, doesn't have the power or the knowledge to change social mores.

I could do it. I didn't perpetuate machismo by teaching a son to command and a daughter to endure. I did it differently with Paula, and especially with Nicolás. What did I want for my daughter? To have options and to live without fear. What did I want for my son? That he be a good companion to women, not an adversary. I didn't impose upon my children the Chilean norm that girls serve the men in the family. Even today I see girls who grow up making their brothers' beds and washing their clothes. Naturally, later on, they become servants to their boyfriends and husbands.

Nicolás learned in the cradle the

concept of gender equality. If I missed some detail, his sister instilled it in him. Now Nicolás is actively engaged in the management of my foundation—the whole purpose of which is to lift up women. He sees on a daily basis the consequences of machismo and he works to alleviate them.

The most revealing opinion was that of Elena, the Honduran woman who cleans my house once a week. She has lived, undocumented, for twenty-two years with her children in the United States. She speaks very little English and lives in fear of being deported at any moment, as happened to her husband, but she manages to support her family. When I asked her if she liked being a woman, she looked at me puzzled. "And what else could I be, **niña** Isabel? God made me this way, so what's the point of complaining?"

This little poll among my friends gave me the idea of asking the same question of my male friends. Do you like being a man? Yes? No? Why? But that would require another fifty pages, so it will have to wait.

———

IN MOST OF THE WORLD, A WOMAN'S value is tied to her youth and beauty. For any woman it's difficult to navigate those waters; for most of us it's a shipwreck. Beauty concerns almost all women in their youth. I barely survived that during the first fifty years of my life, when I thought of myself as not attractive at all. When I was at **Paula** magazine, I compared myself to my colleagues, all of them good-looking, to the fashion models who surrounded us, and to the candidates of the Miss Chile pageant, which we organized annually. What on earth was I thinking? Then I lived in Venezuela, the land of gorgeous and voluptuous women par excellence; they win all the international beauty pageants. Show up at any Venezuelan beach and you'll leave with an incurable inferiority complex.

It's impossible to fit into the mold enforced by the market, the arts, the media, and social mores. By cultivating our low self-esteem, the powers listed above sell us stuff and control us. Objectification of women is so predominant that we don't even perceive it, and in our youth it enslaves us. Feminism has not saved us from that servitude. We can only get rid of it with age, when we become invisible and are no longer objects of desire. Or when a tragedy shakes us to the bone and confronts us with what's essential in life. That happened to me at fifty when my daughter, Paula, died. I applaud the young feminists who are eager to overthrow these stereotypes.

I refuse to submit to the Eurocentric feminine ideal—young, white, tall, thin, and fit—but I celebrate our female instinct to surround ourselves with beauty. We adorn our bodies and we try to adorn our environment. We need harmony. We weave multicolored textiles, we paint murals in mud huts, we make ceramics or lace, we sew—it's universal. Women's creativity is called craft and is sold cheap; when men create, the result is called art and is costly, like Maurizio Cattelan's banana taped to a Miami art gallery wall with a price tag of US$120,000.

In our eagerness to adorn ourselves we are tempted by trinkets or by the illusion that a new shade of lipstick might improve our destiny.

———

AS WITH MANY OTHER SPECIES, HUMAN males are also vain. They spruce themselves up, make noise, and inflate their plumage to attract the best females and sow their seed. The biological imperative of reproduction is implacable. And to that end, beauty plays a fundamental role.

A friend often sends images of exotic birds to my cellphone. Nature's imagination is prodigious when it comes to combining feather colors and shapes. A tiny bird in the Central American jungle sports a rainbow of colors to attract an insignificant-looking female. The male of the species is promiscuous and showy, while the female is plain. Ah, the ironies of evolution! When that bird thinks there's a possible girlfriend around, he chooses a spot with good light and proceeds to clean it meticulously. He removes leaves, twigs, and anything else that might compete with him. Once the stage is ready, he stands in the middle, sings, and magically creates a fan of fluorescent green feathers. The jungle vanishes out of respect for that conceited troubadour.

Humans are sensual creatures; we vibrate in response to sounds, colors, fragrances, textures, flavors—everything that pleases our senses. We are moved not only by the beauty of a planet that offers us that little bird with the green fan, but also by what we can create. Years ago, when my grandchildren were aged five, three, and one, I brought back from a trip to Asia a voluminous wooden crate. We opened it in the living room. Inside, resting on a bed of straw, was a three-foot-tall alabaster statue. It was a serene Buddha, young and svelte, meditating with closed eyes. The kids abandoned their toys and contemplated the statue for a long time, silent and fascinated, as if they understood clearly that this was something extraordinary. Many years later, my grandchildren still bow to the Buddha when they enter my house.

I had the sad task of dismantling my parents' house after they passed away. My mother had managed to buy furniture, ornaments, and good-quality objects in each diplomatic posting. It wasn't easy, because Uncle Ramón had to support four children of his own and three of my mother's, and money was always scarce. Panchita's argument was that refinement is not spontaneously generated and it doesn't come cheap. Each purchase resulted in a fight. The stuff in that house traveled around the world so much that if travel added value, it would have been worth a fortune.

I loved seeing my mother on the stage she had created for herself, like that tiny bird with the green fan. I inherited from her the desire to adorn my house, but I am aware that nothing is permanent, everything changes, decomposes, disintegrates, or dies, so I don't cling to anything.

Trying to give away my parents' belongings, I realized that so much of what she accumulated is no longer valued. There's no time in modern life to shake Persian rugs, polish silver, or wash crystal by hand; nor is there much space for paintings, a grand piano, or antique furniture. Of all that stuff that my mother cared for so much, I kept only a few photographs, a portrait of her painted in Lima when she was a very unhappy young woman, and an old Russian samovar. I now use it to serve tea to my Sisters of Perpetual Disorder—a circle of friends who form a so-called prayer group, although we don't pray at all.

———

ONE TWENTY-FIVE-YEAR-OLD YOUNG woman, the official beauty of her family and among her friends, who has the attitude and confidence to carry that title, once said to me: "I have some advantages. I am tall and I am in better shape than most; I am attractive. However, because of that I am more exposed to harassment. When I was a teenager a man took advantage of me. The sexual abuse and humiliation lasted more than a year. I was afraid of him. Fortunately, my family helped me unconditionally so that I could get out of that toxic relationship. I was weak, inexperienced, and vulnerable, but it was my fault because I was flirtatious and didn't consider the risks."

I stopped her before she could continue along that well-trod path of blaming the victim for a predator's actions. That didn't happen to her because she was pretty; it happened simply because she was female.

———

ACCORDING TO POPULAR MYTH, WOMEN are more vain than men because we worry about our appearance, but male vanity goes deeper and is costlier. Look at their military uniforms and medals, the pomp and solemnity with which they show off, the extreme measures they employ to impress women and make other men envious; their luxurious toys, like cars, and their toys of supremacy, like weapons. I think we can conclude that men and women share the sin of vanity equally.

Panchita was always beautiful and that, we have to admit, is an advantage for women. In photos of her at the age of three, one could already guess the beauty that she would become; photos of her at ninety show undoubtedly that she was still a beauty. In her family, however, physical attributes were never mentioned; it was considered in poor taste. In general, children were not praised; it was a way of keeping them from becoming conceited. If they got good grades in school, they were just doing their duty; if they won the swimming championship, they should have beaten the record; if girls were pretty, they had nothing to boast about and genes were to be thanked. Nothing was enough. That's the way it was in my childhood, and in truth it prepared me for life's harshness. I don't expect to be celebrated. When my grandchildren were little I tried to use this Chilean method on them, but their parents objected; they feared the heartless grandmother would traumatize the kids.

Panchita didn't value the gift of beauty until her mature years. By then she had heard people say she was pretty so often that she ended up believing it. When I took my then fiancé, Roger, now my husband, to Chile to meet my parents, he was impressed by Panchita's looks and told her that she was stunning. She pointed to her husband and answered with a sigh that he had never told her so. Uncle Ramón interjected dryly: "It might be so, but I saw her first."

In the last months of her life, when she needed assistance for everything, even the most intimate tasks, my mother told me that she was resigned to accepting help and that she was grateful for it. "With age and dependency one becomes humble," she confessed. After a thoughtful pause, she added, "But humility does not take away vanity." She dressed with as much elegance as her immobility permitted; her helpers would massage her with lotion in the morning and evening, and a hairdresser turned up twice a week to wash and blow-dry her hair. Her makeup was discreet because, as she would say, there's nothing more ridiculous than a painted old woman. At ninety-something she would look at herself in the mirror and smile. "I don't look bad despite my age, do I? The few friends I have left look like iguanas."

——

I INHERITED MY MOTHER'S VANITY, BUT I kept it hidden in my bones for years, until I was able to get rid of my grandfather's voice making fun of those who pretended to be what they are not. Pretending included lipstick and nail polish because nobody is born with red lips and nails.

At twenty-three I got highlights in my hair, which had recently become fashionable. My grandfather asked me if the cat had urinated on my head. Ashamed, I didn't visit him for several days until he called me to find out what was wrong. He never mentioned the highlights again, and I realized that it wasn't necessary to pay attention to everything he said. Maybe after that incident I started cultivating vanity, not as the sin it was for my **tata,** but as the harmless pleasure it can be if not taken too seriously.

I don't regret having indulged in it since then. But I admit that I have spent energy, time, and money pursuing an ideal until finally I realized that the only reasonable option is to exploit what nature gave me. It isn't much.

I don't have Panchita's physical attributes, so my vanity requires discipline. I jump out of bed an hour before everybody else to shower and put on makeup because when I wake up I look like a defeated boxer. Makeup is miraculous. The right clothes help me conceal the collapse of certain parts of my body; they are down there but I can't find them. I avoid fashion; it's risky. Old photos show me seven months pregnant in a miniskirt and with enough big hair for two wigs. Fashion seldom suits me.

Why such a fuss about my appearance? What about feminism? Because it gives me pleasure. I like fabrics, colors, makeup, and the routine of putting myself together every morning, even though I spend most of my time locked away in the attic writing. "No one sees me, but I see myself," my mother would comment philosophically. She was not referring to her looks only, but also to her deeper character traits and her behavior. It helps me a lot to have a sweetheart who sees me with his heart. My husband, Roger, thinks I am a supermodel, only much shorter.

———

AS THE YEARS GO BY, MY IDEA OF SENSUALITY has shifted. In 1998 I wrote a book about aphrodisiacs, a sort of memoir of the senses that is called, naturally, **Aphrodite,** named for the goddess of love. Aphrodisiacs are those substances that increase desire and sexual performance. Before drugs like Viagra became available, people trusted in certain foods that supposedly had that effect. A good example is eggplant. Turkish brides had to learn dozens of eggplant recipes to guarantee their future husband's enthusiasm for cavorting. I think husbands now prefer a hamburger.

Aphrodisiacs developed in countries like China, Persia, and India, where a man had to satisfy several women. In China, the nation's prosperity could be measured by the number of children the emperor begat. He had hundreds of young concubines for that purpose.

I spent a year researching that book—reading, looking for inspiration in erotic shops, experimenting with aphrodisiac recipes in the kitchen and testing them. Aphrodisiacs are like black magic. I recommend that if you are thinking of using them, you'd better inform the victim if you want results. I learned this when testing my dishes among friends who acted as guinea pigs. The recipe would only work for those guests who had been told that it was an aphrodisiac. I assume that was the case because they left in a hurry. The rest didn't even notice. Suggestion works miracles.

———

BEFORE, I USED TO FANTASIZE ABOUT A night in the company of Antonio Banderas, but now that remote possibility seems like too much work. More sensual is a long shower before lying down with Roger and the dogs between two ironed sheets to watch TV. And for that there's no need to bother with silk lingerie to cover my cellulite.

I was fifty-six years old when I wrote **Aphrodite.** I couldn't write that book now; the subject seems too fanciful, cooking bores me, and I have no intention of administering aphrodisiacs to anybody. I used to say that I couldn't write an erotic book because my mother was still alive. After Panchita passed away, several readers asked me to do it. I am sorry, now it's too late. My mother took too long to bid farewell to this world, and now eroticism interests me way less than kindness and laughter. Maybe I should increase my estrogen dose and start rubbing testosterone cream on my belly.

I wouldn't want to commit again the epic idiocies I engaged in from my thirties into my fifties because of sexual passion, but I don't want to forget them either. They are like merit badges.

I confess, though, that sometimes my passionate heart clouds my understanding. If it's not one of the causes that I obsess over, like justice, the defense of the poor and animals, and, of course, feminism, then usually what clouds my reason is fulminating love. That happened in Venezuela in 1976 when I fell in love with an Argentinian musician who had escaped the so-called Dirty War in his country. I left my good husband and my two children and followed him to Spain. It was a huge mistake and I returned to my family heartbroken and with my tail between my legs. Ten years would pass before my children forgave that betrayal.

That Pied Piper of Hamelin was not the only lover for whom I have done crazy things. On a book tour in 1987, I met Willie, a lawyer from California, and I left my home in Caracas and my children (who by then were adults and didn't need me) and moved without hesitation to live with him, without luggage and without an invitation. Shortly after, I managed to force him into marriage because I needed a visa to be able to sponsor my children so they could come to the United States.

Passion at my age is just as intense as in my youth, but now before doing something reckless I think about it for some time—let's say two or three days. In this way, I let myself be seduced in 2016, when I was seventy-something years old, by a man who crossed my path. It was an impulse of the heart. That was the man who would become my third husband. But I don't want to get ahead of myself. Patience—we will get to Roger soon enough.

My erotic passion is quieter now, and maybe someday it will disappear altogether; I have heard that happens with age. I don't want to think about that possibility right now. If it happens, I hope that passion can be replaced by humor, tenderness, and camaraderie, as some of my older friends who have partners have said. I wonder what could be done if one lover loses passion and libido before the other. I don't know. We'll see if and when the time comes.

Women's emancipation is not incompatible with femininity. Quite the opposite: I think they are complementary. A free spirit can be sexy, depending on the eye of the beholder. I modestly admit that despite feminism I have not lacked wooers during my prolonged existence. I passed through menopause three decades ago and I can still be sexy in private, given certain strategies, of course. In candlelight I might be able to fool a distracted guy who has had three glasses of wine, is not wearing his glasses, and is not intimidated by a woman who takes the initiative.

———

FORTUNATELY, SEXUALITY IS NO LONGER subject to as many rules and classifications. My grandchildren assure me that they are nonbinary. When they introduce me to their friends I now ask each one about their preferred pronouns. It's not easy for me to remember them. I live in California and English is my second language.

This questioning of pronouns started in

the former Yugoslavia, which after terrible wars between 1991 and 2006 was divided into six republics: Slovenia, Croatia, Bosnia-Herzegovina, Montenegro, North Macedonia, and Serbia. In that environment of war and hypermasculinity, patriotism was made up of a mixture of nationalism, patriarchy, and misogyny. Masculinity was defined by power, violence, and conquest. Women and girls from one's own group had to be protected—and impregnated to provide children for the nation. Those on the enemy's side were systematically raped and tortured, both to impregnate the women and humiliate the men. The most conservative estimate is that twenty thousand Bosnian Muslim women were raped by Serbians, but the number could be much higher.

At the end of the conflict, young people questioned gender division imposed by ultranationalism, refused to

be classified as male or female, and rejected the use of gender-based pronouns
in favor of nonbinary ones. This practice
arrived in Europe and the United States
several years later.

Language is very important because it
can determine the way we think. Words
are powerful. Patriarchy benefits from
classifying people; it makes it easier to
exert control. We automatically accept
being placed in categories based on
gender, race, age, etc. But many young
people are challenging these divisions.

Apparently traditional male and female roles have gone out of style; now
one can choose among several alterna-
tives according to one's frame of mind.
Unfortunately, I am fatally heterosexual
and that limits my options. It would be
more convenient to be bisexual or les-
bian because women my age are more
interesting and age better than men.

You think this is an exaggeration? Take a look around.

———

THE DARK FORCES, ESPECIALLY THOSE of religion and tradition, deny women the right to exert their sexuality and pursue pleasure. There are many examples of this: hymen obsession, female fidelity, genital mutilation, etc. Sexual women scare men. A man has to control a woman to make sure that she doesn't have multiple relationships and can't compare him to others or dispense with him entirely. If she seeks pleasure or variety, he cannot be sure of his paternity.

In the West, these forces have retreated some, but they continue to stalk us. I grew up in a time of rampant machismo. Sexual desire and promiscuity were the province of men. It was assumed that females were naturally chaste and had to be seduced. We were not to contribute to our seduction; we had to pretend that we gave in very reluctantly, otherwise we would be labeled "loose." If we relented and the man told others of his triumph, our reputations were stained and we were categorized as a "hussy." Women should not have sexual drives, and any alternative to a monogamous heterosexual relationship was considered an aberration or a sin.

—

Silly, you men—so very adept
at wrongly faulting womankind,
not seeing you're alone to blame
for faults you plant in
    woman's mind.

After you've won by urgent plea
the right to tarnish her
    good name,

you still expect her to behave—
you, that coaxed her into shame.

. . .

So where does the greater
   guilt lie
for a passion that should not be:
with the man who pleads out
   of baseness
or the woman debased by
   his plea?

Or which is more to be blamed—
though both will have cause
   for chagrin:
the woman who sins for money
or the man who pays money
   to sin?

—"SILLY MEN" BY
JUANA INÉS DE LA CRUZ

———

IN MY LIFE I HAVE PROVED TO BE AN incurable romantic, but romance in literature is a huge challenge for me. I have been writing for years without being able to develop the talent of great romance authors; I will never have it. I try to imagine a lover that my heterosexual female readers would like, but that compendium of masculine virtues is beyond my reach. Ideally he is handsome, strong, rich or powerful, not a complete fool, disillusioned by love but ready to fall in love with the female protagonist, etc. I don't know anybody who could serve as my model.

If I manage to come up with a presentable lover—let's say an idealistic and brave young man, all muscle and brown skin, long black hair and velvet eyes, like Huberto Naranjo in **Eva Luna**—he always turns out to be dangerous or slippery; his attraction is often fatal for my female lead, who would end up with a broken heart unless I kill him off on page 159. Sometimes the hero is a good guy, but if he becomes too mushy he also has to die to avoid a sentimental ending. That was the case with Ryan Miller in **Ripper;** I had to choose between killing him or Attila, his dog. What would you have done?

Male lovers in my books are fanatical guerrillas, hair-lipped merchants, vegetarian professors, invisible octogenarians, amputee soldiers, and so on. Among the few exceptions who survived my murderous instinct are Captain Rodrigo de Quiroga and Zorro. The former is a historical character, the valiant conquistador of Chile and Inés Suárez's husband, in my novel **Inés of My Soul.** He escaped my scissors because I didn't invent him; in real life he died in battle when he was already an old man. Zorro isn't my creation either. The masked California hero is more than a hundred years old and still climbing balconies to seduce innocent maidens and bored wives. I can't kill him because the copyright belongs to a corporation that has good lawyers.

My grandchildren have tried to explain to me the numerous forms of love that young people practice today. When they mentioned, for example, polyamorous relationships, I told them that they have always existed. When I was young in the 1960s and 1970s it was called free love, but they assure me that's not the same thing, because many of them are nonbinary—masculine/feminine—and the combinations of partners and groups are much more interesting than in "your time." I hate it when they talk of "your time." This is my time! But I do admit that, unfortunately, I have passed the age in which I could venture into the terrain of modern polyamorous nonbinary relationships.

———

SINCE WE ARE TALKING ABOUT MODERN love, I have to mention dating online, as is done nowadays. In 2015, when my second husband, Willie, and I divorced after twenty-eight years of marriage, I decided to live alone in a small house. To remarry was out of the question. To start again with an old man full of ailments seemed like a nightmare, and to attract a lover was as remote a possibility as growing wings. Nevertheless, some younger friends suggested I should look online. How could I do that if I can't even order something on Amazon? No one would have answered my ad: **Seventy-three-year-old grandmother, documented Latina immigrant, feminist, short of stature and with no**

domestic skills looks for a companion, clean and with good manners, to go to restaurants and movies.

The euphemism for horny is "spontaneous," or something to that effect. I am not spontaneous in the abstract; I need intimacy, dim light, sympathy, and marijuana. For us women, sexual passion diminishes or even disappears as we age unless we are in love. Apparently that's not the case with men. I read somewhere, although it might be a myth, that men think about sex an average of once every three minutes, and they cling to their erotic fantasies up until their death, even if some of them can't remember what an erection is. I wonder how they can get anything done under those circumstances.

Any sixty-year-old grumpy guy with a beer belly feels that he deserves a woman twenty or thirty years younger, as one can see all around, but an older woman with a younger man is still considered obscene. Here's an example of an ad I saw online: **Retired accountant in his seventies, expert in wine and restaurants, looks for busty woman with high libido to have a good time.** Who answers that kind of ad? Since most men want much younger women, if a dupe were to be interested in my profile, he would have to be over a hundred years old.

My journalist's curiosity induced me to research, and I started interviewing women of different ages who had gone online to find a partner. I also investigated a couple of matchmaking agencies, which ended up being fraudulent. For a very high fee they guaranteed eight dates with suitable men. They offered me refined and progressive professionals between sixty-five and seventy-five years of age, in good health, etc. I went out with three or four who matched that description and soon realized that they worked for the agency. The same guys went out with all the clients so that the company could meet its eight-date quota.

The Internet is more honest, although sometimes it lends itself to abuse. Judith, an attractive thirty-year-old woman, waited for her date for forty minutes in a bar. When she gave up and was walking to her car, she got a text message: "I am in the bar but didn't approach you because you are ugly, fat, and old." Why such meanness, I wonder? Judith was depressed for months because of a mentally disturbed jerk who enjoyed bullying a stranger.

———

THIS WAS ANOTHER INTERESTING CASE. Brenda, a pretty, forty-six-year-old, successful businesswoman fell in love online with a romantic and passionate English architect. They were separated by a nine-hour time difference and a ten-hour flying distance, but shared so many common ideas and inclinations it was as if they had grown up together. The architect and Brenda had the same tastes, from classical music to Persian cats. He tried to travel to California to meet her on a couple of occasions, but his work prevented him from doing so. She wanted to go to London, but he insisted that he needed to see her in her environment, in her house, with her friends and her show cats. Finally they agreed to meet when he returned from Turkey, where he had an important project.

Soon after, Brenda got a call from a lawyer. The architect had run over a person while driving a rented car in Istanbul. He had been arrested and was desperate; the conditions in the prison were a nightmare and he urgently needed a loan to make bail. The money had to be deposited immediately in a specific bank account.

Brenda was very much in love, but she was not stupid. The figure was very high, even for someone with as many resources as she had, and before wiring the money she consulted a local detective. "Look, lady. I am not going to charge you because I don't need to investigate this case, I know it by heart," the detective said, and explained that the guy was a well-known swindler, an unemployed actor from Los Angeles who specialized in deceiving lonely and wealthy women on the Internet. He found out as much as possible about them in order to present himself as the ideal suitor. Brenda had a very informative webpage and he got the rest by using his aristocratic British accent during their long conversations. He seduced her as he had done before with several other women.

She did not send him the money for the supposed bail and never heard from him again. Her disappointment was so great that she couldn't even lament the loss of love; instead, she was grateful to have been saved in time. According to her, the moral of the story was that one shouldn't trust English architects.

I am not as smart as Brenda. I would have gotten the money he requested and would have traveled that same night to Turkey to rescue the man from his dungeon. Fortunately, I didn't have to take any of those risks. And I am not alone either, as I had envisioned, because heaven sent me a troubadour I was not expecting.

———

WE HAVE TALKED ABOUT SEXUAL PASSION and romantic passion. But what does it mean simply to be passionate? According to the dictionary, it's a disorderly mood disturbance; it is also described as a powerful and irresistible emotion that can lead to obsessive or dangerous actions.

My own definition is less somber. Passion is unbridled enthusiasm, exuberant energy, and determined devotion to someone or something. The good thing about passion is that it pushes us forward and keeps us committed and young. I have been training for years to be a passionate old woman, just as others train to climb mountains or play chess. I don't want to allow caution, so often prevalent in later years, to destroy my passion for life.

Almost all the female protagonists of my books are passionate because they are the people who interest me. I want characters capable of committing obsessive and dangerous actions, as the dictionary says. A safe and quiet life is not good material for fiction.

I have sometimes been described as a passionate person because I never sat quietly in my house, as was expected of me. I have to clarify that my risky endeavors were motivated not always by a passionate temperament but because circumstances threw me in unexpected directions. I did the best I could. I have lived in a rough sea where waves would lift me and then drop me to the bottom. This surge has been so strong that before, when things went well, I would prepare for a violent fall, which I considered inevitable, instead of relaxing in the tranquillity of the moment. Now it's not like that. Now I drift along day after day, happy just to float for as long as possible.

———

THOUGH I ALWAYS HAD PASSION WHEN I was a young woman, I don't think I had literary ambition. I think the idea never crossed my mind because ambition was a male thing; when applied to women it was an insult. The Women's Liberation Movement allowed some women to appropriate this concept, just as they did with assertiveness, competitiveness, desire for power, eroticism, and the self-confidence to say no. Once in a while the women of my generation grabbed the opportunities that were available—not that there were many—but we rarely had a plan for success.

In the absence of ambition I had good luck. Nobody, let alone I, could foresee the immediate acceptance that I enjoyed with my first novel and have experienced with the rest of my books. Maybe my grandmother was right when she prophesied that her granddaughter was going to be fortunate because I had a birthmark in the shape of a star on my back. For years I thought that birthmark was unique, but as it happens it's very common, and moreover it fades over time.

I was always disciplined in my work because I internalized my grandfather's admonition that leisure time was dead time. I followed that rule for decades, but I have learned that leisure can be fertile soil where creativity grows. I am no longer tormented by an excess of discipline, as I was before. Now I write for the pleasure of telling a story word by word, step by step, enjoying the process without thinking of the result. I don't tie myself to a chair eight or ten hours a day, writing with the concentration of a notary. I can relax because I have the rare privilege of having loyal readers and good publishers who don't try to influence my work.

I write about what I care for, in my own rhythm. In those leisure hours that my grandfather considered wasted, the ghosts of imagination become well-defined characters. They are unique, they have their own voices, and they are willing to tell me their stories if I give them enough time. I feel them around me with such certitude that I wonder why nobody else perceives them.

The ability to overcome obsessive discipline didn't happen in one day; it took me years. In therapy and in my minimal spiritual practice I learned to tell my superego to back off and leave me alone; I want to enjoy my freedom. Superego is not the same as consciousness; the former punishes us and the latter guides us. I stopped listening to the overseer inside me who demands compliance and performance with the voice of my grandfather. The race uphill is over; now I stroll calmly in the land of intuition, which has turned out to be the best environment for writing.

———

MY FIRST NOVEL, THE HOUSE OF THE Spirits, was published in 1982 after the boom in Latin American literature, as the set of magnificent books written by a group of famous writers from my continent was called. The boom was a male phenomenon. Women writers in Latin America were systematically ignored by critics, professors, students of literature, and publishing houses. If they were published at all, it was in small editions without adequate promotion or distribution. The reception my novel got surprised everybody. It was said that it had taken the literary world by storm. Wow! Suddenly it became obvious that the readers of novels were mostly women, and not just in Latin America. There was an important market out there, just waiting for publishing houses to grab it. That's exactly what they did, and now as much fiction is published by women as by male writers.

And this is where I have to pay posthumous tribute to Carmen Balcells, another of the passionate and remarkable women who helped me along the journey of my life. Carmen, a famous literary agent from Barcelona, was the godmother of almost all the great writers of this Latin American boom, as well as of hundreds of other Spanish-language authors. She spied some merit in my first novel and she had it published, first in Spain and then in many other countries. Whatever I have achieved in this strange craft of writing I owe to her.

I was an unknown person who had written her first little novel in the kitchen of her apartment in Caracas. Carmen invited me to Barcelona for the launch of the book. She didn't know me at all, but she treated me like a celebrity. She threw a party in her house to introduce me to the city's intellectual elite, critics, journalists, and writers. I didn't know a soul. I was dressed like a hippie and was totally out of place, but she calmed me with just one sentence: "Here nobody knows more than you; we all improvise." That reminded me of Uncle Ramón's advice: **Remember that everybody is more scared than you are.**

That dinner party was the only occasion where I have seen Russian caviar served with a soup ladle. At the table Carmen raised her glass to toast my book, and at that very moment the electricity went out and we were left in pitch darkness. Without a moment's hesitation, as if she had rehearsed it, Carmen said: "This Chilean woman's spirits have come to toast with us! Cheers!"

———

CARMEN WAS MY MENTOR AND MY friend. She used to say that we were not friends; I was her client and she was my agent, that we only had a business relationship, but that was not true at all. (Nor was her proclamation that she would have liked to be a kept woman. I can't imagine anybody less gifted for that role than she.) Carmen was at my side during my most significant moments, from Paula's illness to family weddings to my divorces, always supporting me unconditionally, always present.

This woman, who was able to confront the biggest bully, consulted an astrologer; she believed in psychics, gurus, and magic. She would easily get emotional and cry. She cried so much that Gabriel García Márquez dedicated one of his books to her: **To Carmen Balcells, bathed in tears.**

She was generous to an extreme. For my mother's eightieth birthday, she sent eighty white roses all the way to Chile, and when Uncle Ramón turned ninety-nine she did the same for him. She never forgot his birthday because they were born the same day in August. Once she gave me a complete set of Louis Vuitton luggage because she considered mine cheap and old. It was stolen at the airport in Caracas the first and only time I used it, but I didn't tell her because she would have replaced it immediately. She would send me so many chocolates that I still find some hidden in the most unexpected corners of my house.

After the sudden death of this formidable Catalan lady, I had the feeling for a while that I had lost the life vest that kept me afloat in the stormy literary sea. But the agency she created with her talent and vision continues smoothly under the management of her son, Lluís Miquel Palomares.

I have Carmen's photograph on my desk to remind me of her advice: Anybody can write a good first book, but a writer is proved by the second and by those that follow; you are going to be judged harshly because success in women is not easily forgiven; write what you want; don't allow anybody to interfere with your work or in the handling of your money; treat your children like royalty, they deserve it; get married, because a husband, no matter if he is a moron, looks good.

Just as Carmen warned me, it has taken me decades to get the recognition that any male author in my situation would take for granted. It has been very hard to achieve acceptance with Chilean critics, but I have always had my readers' affection. I don't hold a grudge about the bad reviews because criticism is a national trait; in Chile anybody who rises too far above average is crushed, with the notable exception of soccer players. We have a noun and a verb for this: **chaqueteo** and **chaquetear,** which mean to grab someone by the lapels and pull him or her down. If the victim is female, the cruelty and speed are doubled to prevent her from becoming too confident. If I didn't suffer from this **chaqueteo** I would worry; it would mean that I am of no importance whatsoever.

After I had published twenty books, which have been translated into forty-something languages, a Chilean writer whose name I don't remember said that I was not a writer, I was a typist. Carmen Balcells asked him if he had formed his opinion based on having read any of my work. His reply: "Over my dead body." This was when I was nominated for the National Prize for Literature. In 2010, with the support of four former presidents, several political parties, and Congress, I received the award. Only then did I finally win some respect from Chilean critics. Carmen sent me ten pounds of orange peels covered in dark chocolate, my favorite.

———

MAE WEST, THE BLACK-AND-WHITE-movie diva, said that one is never too old to get younger. Love rejuvenates, there's no doubt about that. I am enjoying a new love and maybe that's why I feel as healthy and enthusiastic as if I were thirty years younger. In my case it's an excess of endorphins, the happiness hormones. It seems that we all feel younger than our chronological years and are surprised when the calendar reminds us that another year or another decade has gone by. Time slips by quickly. I tend to forget my age so completely that I am baffled when I am offered a seat on the bus.

I feel young because I can still roll on the floor with the dogs, sneak out for ice cream, remember what I had for breakfast, and make love laughing. But to be prudent, I don't test my abilities and I quietly accept my limitations. I do less than I did before and ration my time because any task takes me longer. I refuse unappealing commitments, which

I agreed to before out of duty, such as unnecessary trips and social gatherings of more than eight people, where I disappear, finding myself staring at the waists of other, taller guests. I avoid noisy children and bad-tempered adults.

With age we suffer more losses; it's only natural. We lose people, pets, places, and the unstoppable energy of youth. Until I turned seventy I could juggle three or four tasks simultaneously, work several days with minimal sleep, and write nonstop for ten hours. I was flexible and strong. I could jump out of bed at dawn, throwing both legs in the air and landing with some semblance of grace on the floor, ready to shower and start the day. Lingering in bed? Lazy Sundays? **Siesta?** None of that for me. Now I crawl out of bed, careful not to bother my partner and the dogs. I have only one obligation—to write—and it takes me forever to get started. I can do it for no more than four or five hours and only with lots of coffee and willpower.

———

THE DESIRE FOR YOUTH HAS ALWAYS existed. The first known mention of the fountain of eternal youth is from Herodotus in the fifth century B.C. The greedy Spaniards and Portuguese who conquered Latin America in the sixteenth century searched for El Dorado, the city of pure gold where kids played marbles with emeralds and rubies, and the Fountain of Youth, whose waters erased the ravages of age. They didn't find either. Nobody believes in El Dorado any longer, but the mirage of eternal youth persists, today sustained by an arsenal of resources for those who can afford them—drugs, vitamins, diets, exercise, surgery, and even injections of placenta and human plasma that would delight Dracula.

I suppose all of it is useful because we now live thirty years longer than our grandparents. But living longer doesn't mean living better. In fact, a prolonged old age exacts a huge social and economic cost on both individuals and the planet.

———

DAVID SINCLAIR, A PROFESSOR OF genetics at Harvard Medical School and the author of several books, maintains that aging is a pathology and needs to be treated as such. His molecular experiments have stopped, and in some cases reversed, aging in rats. He says that the technology already exists. In the near future we will be able to avoid the symptoms and illnesses of old age by eating mostly plants and taking a pill at breakfast. In theory we could live to be one hundred and twenty years old, in good health and with a clear mind.

For the time being, until Sinclair moves from rats to humans, maybe the secret of prolonged youth is attitude, as my mother used to say, and Sophia Loren, the movie goddess of the 1950s to the 1970s, confirmed. I mentioned Sophia to my grandchildren (now all adults) and they had no idea who she was. I am not surprised; they didn't know who Gandhi was either. I met Sophia at the Olympic Winter Games in Italy in 2006 when we and six other women carried the Olympic flag through the stadium.

Sophia stood out like a peacock among chickens. I couldn't take my eyes off her. She had been the sex symbol of an era, and at seventy-something was still stunning. What is the secret of her invincible attraction and youth? In a TV interview she said the secret was happiness, and that all one can see, she owes to spaghetti. In another interview she added that the trick was to maintain good posture. "I am always straight and I don't make old people noises, no panting, complaining, coughing, or shuffling." Attitude is her mantra. I follow Sophia's advice about posture, but not that nonsense about spaghetti. I tried it once and gained ten pounds.

There's nothing wrong with aging except that Mother Nature discards the old ones. Once the reproductive years are over and we are done raising our offspring, we are disposable. Maybe in some remote places, like a hypothetical village in Borneo, age is venerated and no one wants to look any younger because it's preferable to look older if one is to be respected. That's not so in our case. Nowadays, ageism is politically incorrect, as sexism and racism have been for decades, but nobody pays any attention. There's a monumental anti-aging industry, as if aging were a character flaw.

In the past, adulthood arrived at twenty, middle age at forty, and old age at fifty. Today adolescence lasts until past thirty or forty, maturity comes around sixty, and old age starts at eighty. This is the baby boomers' achievement. Over the last half century they have redefined many cultural aspects for their convenience.

In any case, even if we cling to the illusion of youth, most people my age are striding toward decrepitude and we are all going to end up dead before prejudice against aging is abolished.

I will not be able to enjoy the advances of science, but it's likely my grandchildren will reach a hundred years of age in good shape. I'm content to age cheerfully, and to that end I apply some simple rules: I no longer acquiesce easily; goodbye to stiletto heels, diets, and patience with fools; I have learned to say no to what I dislike without feeling guilty. Now my life is better, but I am not interested in the warrior's rest; I'd rather keep some ardency of mind and blood.

———

MORE THAN SPAGHETTI AND POSTURE, AS Sophia Loren recommends, my secret for a full life and happy old age is to emulate my friend Olga Murray. Imagine a young lady ninety-four years old who doesn't wear eyeglasses or hearing aids, doesn't use a walking stick, dresses in striking colors and tennis shoes, and still drives her car, but only forward and without changing lanes. This diminutive, energetic, and passionate woman has a purpose that guides her journey, fills her days, and keeps her young.

Her story is fascinating, but I will have to summarize it here. (Please find Olga Murray online. It's worth it.) After becoming a widow in her sixties, Olga decided to trek in the mountains of Nepal, where she fell and broke an ankle. The Sherpa who accompanied her had to carry her in a basket on his back to the closest village, which turned out to be very poor and isolated. There, while she waited for transportation to the city, Olga witnessed a festival. The villagers prepared food with the little they had and dressed in their best clothes, and there was music and dancing. Soon agents came in buses from the cities to buy little girls between the ages of six and eight. Their fathers sold them because they could not afford to feed them.

The agents paid the equivalent of two goats or a piglet and took the girls away, after promising the parents that their daughters would live with good families, go to school, and eat well. Instead, the girls were sold as **kamlaris,** a form of bondage similar to slavery. **Kamlaris** worked nonstop, slept on the floor, ate the family's leftovers, and had no education or healthcare. Those were the fortunate ones. The others were sold to brothels.

Olga realized that even if she used all her money to buy a couple of girls, she could not give them back to their families because they would be sold again, but she was determined to help the **kamlaris.** That became her life's mission. She knew she would have to care for the girls she could rescue for several years, until they could fend for themselves. She returned to California and created a charitable organization called the Nepal Youth Foundation (nepalyouthfoundation.org) to provide housing, education, and healthcare to exploited children. Olga has saved some fifteen thousand girls from domestic bondage. She has also managed to change Nepal's culture. Thanks to her, the Nepalese government has declared the **kamlari** practice illegal.

Olga has other similarly spectacular programs—several homes for orphans and abandoned children, and schools and nutritional clinics attached to hospitals, where mothers are trained to feed their families tasty, well-balanced meals with the resources they have. I have seen the before-and-after pictures. A famished kid, just skin and bones, who couldn't even walk, is playing with a ball a month later.

Olga's foundation built a model village on the outskirts of Kathmandu. It has a school, several workshops, and housing for vulnerable kids. The name is perfect for the place: Olgapuri, Olga's oasis. How I wish you could see it! This marvelous woman is adored by thousands of children in Nepal, and it's not an overstatement when I say thousands.

When she arrives at the Kathmandu airport, there is always a crowd of kids and young people with balloons and garlands to welcome their mama.

At her late age Olga is so healthy and strong that she travels a couple of times a year back and forth from Nepal to California, twenty hours. She works nonstop to fundraise for and supervise her projects. Her blue eyes shine passionately when she talks about her kids. She is always smiling, always cheerful. I have never heard her complain or place blame; she is all kindness and gratitude. Olga Murray is my heroine. When I grow up, I want to be just like her.

——

I WOULD LIKE TO HAVE SOPHIA LOREN'S full breasts and long legs, but if given a choice, I prefer the gifts of several good witches I know: purpose, compassion, and good humor.

According to the Dalai Lama, the only hope for peace and prosperity lies in the hands of women in the West. I suppose it's because they have more rights and resources than others, but I would not exclude the rest of the women in the world. The task belongs to all of us.

For the first time in history there are millions of educated women who are informed, connected, and determined to change the civilization in which we live. We are not alone; many men are with us in this, almost all young—our sons and grandsons.

This is the era of emboldened grandmothers, and we are the population's fastest-growing group. We are women who have lived long lives; we have nothing to lose and therefore are not easily scared; we can speak up because we don't care to compete, to please, or to be popular; and we know the immense value of friendship and collaboration. We are anxious about the situation of humanity and the planet. Now it's a matter of agreeing to give the world a formidable shake.

———

RETIREMENT IS ANOTHER THING THAT increasingly concerns women, because most of us now work outside the home. Homemakers, however, never retire and never rest. In Spanish, the word for retirement is **jubilación,** a word that comes from **jubilance** because retirement is supposed to be an ideal time when one can do as one pleases. That's wishful thinking. Too often retirement comes when body and budget don't allow us to do what we want. Also, it's a proven fact that free time doesn't mean happier time.

Retirement for men can be the beginning of the end because they value themselves in relation to their work.

They invest in their jobs everything they are as people, and when work ends, they have very little left and they sink mentally and emotionally. That is when the worst fears hit hardest: fear of failure, fear of losing economic resources, fear of being alone, and so on—the list is long. If a man doesn't have a caring partner or a dog who wags its tail every time it sees him, he is finished. Women fare better because aside from working, we have cultivated friendships and family relationships; we are more sociable than men and have more diverse interests. However, the fragility that comes with aging also makes us fearful. I am generalizing, but you get it.

According to Gerald G. Jampolsky, a famous psychiatrist and the author of many bestsellers about psychology and philosophy, an aptitude for happiness is determined 45 percent by genes and

15 percent by circumstances. That means that the remaining 40 percent is based on our beliefs and attitude about life. Even at ninety-five, Jampolsky is still seeing patients and writing; he goes to the gym five days a week, and every morning when he wakes up he gives thanks for the new day and commits to live it happily, no matter his physical state. Age should not limit our energy or creativity or our willingness to participate in the world.

Now that we live longer, we have a couple of decades ahead of us to redefine our goals and find meaning in the years to come. Jampolsky recommends letting go of grievances and negativity. More energy is needed to sustain ill feelings than to forgive. The key to contentment is forgiveness of others and of ourselves. Our last years can be the best if we opt for love instead of fear, he says.

Love doesn't grow like a wild plant, it needs a lot of care.

———

QUESTION FROM A JOURNALIST TO THE Dalai Lama: Can you remember your past lives?

Answer: At my age it's hard to remember what happened yesterday.

———

UNCLE RAMÓN, MY STEPFATHER, WAS A very active and brilliant man until he left his job as director of the Diplomatic Academy in Chile; that's when his decline started. He was very sociable and had dozens of friends, but one by one they became senile or passed away. In addition, his siblings and one of his daughters died. In his last years—he reached the venerable age of 102—he had only the company of Panchita, who by then was quite tired of his bad temper and would have preferred to be a widow. A team of kind women took care of him as if he were a greenhouse orchid.

"My biggest mistake was to retire. I was eighty but that's just a number. I could have gone on working another ten years," he told me once. I didn't find it in me to remind him that at eighty he needed help to tie his shoes, but I agree that his slow downward slope began when he retired.

This has strengthened my decision to be active forever and use every brain cell and soul spark so there will be nothing left when I go. I am not going to retire, I am going to renovate. I am not willing to be cautious. According to Julia Child, the celebrity chef, the secret of her longevity was red meat and gin. My excesses are different but, like Julia, I will not give them up. My mother used to say that the only regrets in our old age are the sins we didn't commit and the things we didn't buy.

Unless dementia defeats me, which has not yet happened among my long-lived relatives, I don't intend to become a passive old woman with only a dog or two for company. That's a very scary proposition, but as Jampolsky says, we shouldn't live in fear. I am preparing for the future. With age, defects and virtues are exacerbated; we become more of what we always were. If we were nasty at forty, we will not be kind at eighty, we will probably be detestable. It is not true that as we age we become wiser, quite the opposite; usually old people are a little mad. If we aspire to wisdom, we have to start training at a young age, as my mother used to say. For as long as possible I will crawl up the stairs to the attic where I write and spend my days entertained by telling stories. If

I can achieve that, old age is none of my business.

—

SOCIETY DETERMINES THE THRESHOLD of old age—when we can legally retire and collect a pension. At that age most people retire, women let their hair go gray (don't do it yet!), and men use Viagra to pursue their fantasies (how awful!). In reality, aging starts at birth and each person experiences it differently. Culture has a lot to do with this. At fifty a woman in Las Vegas might be invisible, but in Paris she might still be very attractive. At seventy a man might be ancient in some remote village, but in the San Francisco Bay Area, where I live, one can see gangs of grandfathers on bikes, which would be praiseworthy if they didn't wear tight shorts in fluorescent colors.

They tell us that exercise and diet are essential if we are to age in good shape.

That might be so, but we shouldn't generalize. I was never athletic so I see no reason to kill myself exercising this late in life. I keep myself fit walking the dogs to the closest coffee shop for my daily cappuccino. My parents lived quite healthily for a century and I never saw them sweating in a gym or limiting their food intake. They had a glass or two of wine at mealtimes and a cocktail in the evening. They consumed cream, butter, red meat, eggs, coffee, dessert, and all sorts of prohibited carbohydrates. All in moderation. They were not overweight and had never heard of cholesterol.

My parents had love and care up until the last days of their splendid lives. That's very rare. The last stage of life is usually tragic because society is not prepared to deal with longevity. No matter how carefully laid out our plans might be, generally our resources don't last until the end. The last six years of our lives are usually the most expensive, painful, and lonely; these are years of dependency, and with terrible frequency they are years of poverty. The family—more specifically, the women in the family—took care of the elderly in the past, but in this part of the world that's not the case anymore. Houses are small, money is short, work and the rhythms of life are demanding, and to top it off, grandparents live too long.

Those of us who have reached our seventh decade are terrified of ending our days in a nursing home, in diapers, drugged, and tied to a wheelchair. I want to die before I need help to take a shower. My women friends and I dream of creating a community. (I just got married and don't want to think about widowhood; it's depressing, but we are assuming, of course, that one day we will be widows because men die earlier.) For example, we could buy a plot somewhere not too far from a hospital and build individual cabins with common services, a place where we could have our pets, a garden, and some fun. We talk about it often but we keep postponing it, not only because it's a costly proposition but also because deep inside we believe we will always be independent. Magical thinking.

———

UNLESS WE CAN AVOID THE SYMPTOMS of aging and remain healthy until we are a hundred and twenty, as Professor Sinclair proposes, we have to deal with the tricky subject of longevity. It's foolish to keep avoiding it. Society needs to find a way to care for the elderly and to help them die if they so desire. Assisted death should be a viable option everywhere, not only in a few enlightened places on earth. Death with dignity is a human right, but the law and the medical establishment often force us to live way beyond dignity. As Abraham Lincoln supposedly said, "And in the end, it's not the years in your life that count, it's the life in your years."

I had an agreement with a male friend, who at eighty-five is still the seductive stud that he always was, to commit suicide together when we deemed it appropriate. He was going to fly his plane—a tin mosquito—toward the horizon until we had no more fuel and then we would plunge into the Pacific Ocean, a clean ending that would spare our families the cost of two funerals. Unfortunately, a couple of years ago, my friend's pilot license expired and he could not renew it. He had to sell his mosquito. Now he is thinking of buying a motorcycle. That's what I wish for myself, a quick death, because I am not Olga Murray and don't have my own village of kind people to take care of me at the end.

By the way, as the birth rate continues

to drop and the population gets older in the United States and Europe, immigrants should be welcomed with open arms. They are young—the elderly don't emigrate—and their work helps support retirees. Also, it is female immigrants who traditionally take care of children and old people. They are the patient and kind nannies of those we love most.

The elderly are treated not as a priority but as a nuisance. The government doesn't assign them enough resources; the healthcare system is unfair and inadequate; living quarters in most cases consist of warehousing old people away from the public eye. The country should support, in a decent manner, those who contributed to society for forty or fifty years. But that's not the case, unless we are talking about some exceptionally civilized country, one of those where we would all like to live. The terrible fate of most old people is to end up dependent, poor, and rejected.

———

MAYBE MY PLAN TO REMAIN ACTIVE AND die with my boots on will fail. Maybe there will be a moment when I will have to abdicate bit by bit what I now consider important. I hope the last things to go will be writing and sensuality.

If I live too long I will lose my capacity to pay attention. If I am not able to remember and focus I will not be able to write, and then everybody around me will suffer. For them, the ideal situation is for me to be absent and, if possible, isolated in a closed room. If I lose my mind I won't even notice, but if I lose independence while totally lucid, as happened to my mother, it will be rather disagreeable.

I still have total mobility, but the day will come when I will not be able to drive anymore. I have always been a lousy driver and now I am worse. I crash into trees that suddenly appear where there was nothing before. I avoid driving at night because I cannot read the street signs and I end up irrevocably lost. Driving is not the only challenge. I refuse to update my computer, replace my cellphone, exchange my old car, or learn to use our TV's five remote controls. I can't open bottles, chairs have become heavier, buttonholes smaller, and shoes tighter.

Sensuality changes as we age. My friend Grace Damman, one of the six Sisters of Perpetual Disorder, my intimate spiritual practice circle, has spent many years in a wheelchair following a terrible head-on collision on the Golden Gate Bridge. She was very athletic and was training to climb Mount Everest before the accident, which pulverized her bones and left her semi-paralyzed. It took her years to accept her physical condition; in her mind she was still waterskiing in Hawaii and running marathons.

Grace is in a residence for older people because she needs assistance; she is by far the youngest person there. The help she gets is not much, just five minutes in the morning to dress her, five minutes in the evening to put her to bed, and two showers a week. For her, the greatest pleasure is that shower. She says that every drop of water on her skin is a blessing; she enjoys the soap and shampoo foam in her hair. I often think of Grace when I shower; I don't want to take that privilege for granted.

———

WHILE MY BODY DETERIORATES, MY SOUL rejuvenates. I suppose my defects and virtues are also more visible. I spend and waste too much and am more distracted than before, but I also have become less angry; my character has softened a little. My passion for the causes I have always embraced and for those few people I love has increased. I do not fear my vulnerability because I no longer confuse it with weakness. I can live with my arms, doors, and heart open. This is another good reason to celebrate my age and my gender: I don't have to prove my masculinity, as Gloria Steinem said. That is, I don't have to cultivate the image of fortitude instilled by my grandfather, which was very useful earlier in my life but not anymore; now I can ask for help and be sentimental.

Since my daughter died I am perfectly aware of death's proximity; and now, in my seventies, death is my friend. It's not true that she looks like a skeleton armed with a scythe and trailed by a rotten odor; she is a mature and elegant lady who smells of gardenias. At first she was lurking in the neighborhood, then in the house next door, and now she is waiting patiently in my garden. Sometimes, when I pass in front of her, we greet each other and she reminds me that I should enjoy this day as if it were my last.

In brief, I am in a splendid moment of my destiny. This is good news for women in general: Life gets easier once we get through menopause and are done with raising kids, but only if we minimize our expectations, give up resentment, and relax in the knowledge that no one, except those closest to us, gives a damn about who we are or what we do. Stop pretending, faking it, lamenting, and flagellating ourselves about silly stuff. We have to love ourselves a lot and love others without calculating how much we are loved in return. This is the stage of kindness.

THE EXTRAORDINARY WOMEN I HAVE met in my life nurtured the vision I had when I was fifteen years old of a world where feminine values carry the same weight as masculine ones, just as I used to preach to my grandfather, who listened with pursed lips and white knuckles. "I don't know what world you live in, Isabel. You talk about stuff that has nothing to do with us," he would argue. He repeated that years later when the military coup put an end to our democracy in just a few hours, and the country was subjected to a long dictatorship.

Being a journalist I knew what was going on in the shadows: concentration camps, torture centers, thousands of **desaparecidos**—murdered people whose bodies were dynamited in the desert or thrown from helicopters into the sea.

My grandfather didn't want to know; he insisted that those were just rumors, that none of it was of my concern. He commanded me to stay out of politics, to be quiet at home, to think about my husband and my children. "Remember the story of the parrot who wanted to stop the train by flapping his wings? The train tore it to pieces, not even the feathers remained. Is that what you want?"

That rhetorical question has haunted me for decades. What do I want? What do women want? Allow me to remind you of the ancient story of the caliph.

Once, in the mythical city of Baghdad, a thief was brought in front of the caliph to be judged. The usual punishment was to have his hands cut off, but that day the caliph was in a good mood and he offered the bandit a way out. "Tell me what women want and you will be free," he said. The man thought for a while, and after invoking Allah and His Prophet, he gave the caliph an astute answer. "Oh, sublime caliph, women want to be heard. Ask them what they want and they will tell you."

While writing this part of the book I thought I needed to research some more, but instead of going around interrogating women here and there about their wishes, I could save time consulting the Internet. I typed out the caliph's riddle, "What do women want?" Google responded with self-help manuals with titles like "Find out what women want and fuck them." I also got advice from men instructing other men how to score. Here's an example: **Women want tough guys, be aggressive and confident, don't give them any power, order them around, be demanding, your needs have priority, that's what they like.**

Is that so? I doubt it. It's not true

among the women I know, who are many if I count my loyal readers and those I work with at my foundation. I think I might have a better answer to the caliph's inquiry.

This is what women want: to be safe, to be valued, to live in peace, to have their own resources, to be connected, to have control over their bodies and lives, and above all, to be loved. In the next few pages, I will try to explain what this entails.

———

THE MOST SIGNIFICANT INDICATOR OF the level of violence in a nation is its rate of violence against women, which normalizes all other forms of violence. In Mexico, where there is insecurity in the streets, and cartels and organized criminal gangs act with impunity, approximately ten women are murdered daily. This is a conservative estimate. Most of the victims are beaten or killed at the hands of boyfriends, husbands, and other men they know. Since the 1990s hundreds of young women in Ciudad Juárez, Chihuahua, have been killed after being raped and often brutally tortured. The government has responded with indifference. This elicited a massive women's protest in March 2020. Women declared a general strike: They didn't go to work, they didn't do any domestic chores, and hundreds of thousands marched in the streets. We'll see if this has any impact on the authorities.

The Democratic Republic of the Congo, which has a history of instability and armed conflict, holds the shameful title of "rape capital of the world." Rape and other forms of systematic aggression against women are weapons of oppression used by armed groups; one in three assaults, however, are inflicted by civilians. The situation in other places in

Africa, in Latin America, in the Middle East, and in Asia is also bad. The greater the hypermasculinity and gender polarization, the more violence women suffer, as is the case among terrorist groups.

We want safety for ourselves and our children. We are programmed to defend our kids and we do that with claws and determination. That's also the case with most animals, although I'm not so sure about reptiles, like snakes and crocodiles. With few exceptions, the mother cares for her offspring, and sometimes she is forced to protect them with her life against a hungry male who might devour them.

When threatened, the male reaction is flight or fight: adrenaline and testosterone. When threatened, the female reaction is to form a circle and put the offspring in the middle: oxytocin and estrogen. Oxytocin, the hormone that drives us to unite, is so amazing that some psychiatrists use it in couples therapy. The partners inhale oxytocin with a nasal spray, hoping to reach agreement instead of murdering each other. Willie and I tried it but it didn't quite work; maybe we didn't inhale enough. Eventually we divorced, but the residue of that blessed hormone allowed us to remain good friends until his recent death. Proof of our friendship is that Willie left me Perla, his little dog. She is the unfortunate product of several different breeds; she has the face of a bat and the body of a fat rat, but she has a great personality.

——

VIOLENCE AGAINST WOMEN IS UNIVERSAL and as old as civilization. When talking about human rights, in truth we're referring to men's rights. If a man is beaten and deprived of his freedom, it's called torture. When a woman endures the same, it's called domestic violence and is still considered a private matter in most of the world. In some places, murdering a woman over a matter of honor is not even reported. The United Nations estimates that every year around five thousand girls and women in the Middle East and Asia are killed to protect a man's or a family's honor.

A woman is raped every six minutes in the United States. That's counting only the cases that are reported; in reality the number is estimated to be at least five times higher. And every nine seconds a woman is beaten. Harassment and intimidation happen at home, in the streets, in the workplace, and on social media where anonymity encourages the worst forms of misogyny. And we are just talking about the United States here; imagine how it is in other countries where women's rights are still in diapers. Such violence is inherent to the patriarchy; it is not an abnormality. It's time to call it out for what it is and speak up.

—

TO BE A WOMAN MEANS TO LIVE IN FEAR. Every woman has a fear of men in her DNA. She thinks twice before doing something as routine as walking past a group of men. In places that are supposedly safe, like a university campus or a military institution, there are programs that teach women to avoid risky situations, and then assume that if she is attacked it is her fault. She was in the wrong place at the wrong time. Men are not expected to change their behavior. Moreover, sexual aggression is not only allowed, it is even celebrated as a man's right and proof of his masculinity. Fortunately this is rapidly changing, at least in first-world countries, thanks to #MeToo and other feminist initiatives.

An extreme expression of the above are

women who live buried in burkas that cover them from head to toe to avoid sparking male desire. Apparently, men have bestial impulses that are triggered by the sight of an inch of female skin or a white sock. That is to say, women are punished for men's weakness and vice. I recognize that some women choose to wear a burka because they are religiously observant. That said, some women fear men so much that they defend the use of the burka on the grounds that it allows them to be invisible, and therefore safer. The truth is that all human beings should feel safe in this world.

The author Eduardo Galeano said that "in the end, women's fear of men's violence is a reflection of men's fear of women without fear." Sounds good but the concept seems confusing to me. How could we not be afraid if the world colludes to scare us? There are very few fearless women, except when we get together. In a group we feel invincible.

What's at the root of this explosive mixture of desire for and hatred of women? Why are aggression and harassment not civil rights or human rights concerns? Why are women silenced? Why isn't there a declared war against such violence, like the war against drugs, terrorism, or crime? The answer is obvious: Violence and fear are instruments of control.

———

BETWEEN 2005 AND 2009 IN THE ULTRA-conservative and remote Mennonite colony of Manitoba in Bolivia, one hundred and fifty women and girls, including a little girl only three years old, were repeatedly raped after being drugged with a spray used to anesthetize bulls prior to castration. They would wake up bruised and bloody and the explanation given by the elders was that they were being punished by the Devil, that they were the victims of demonic possession. The women and girls were illiterate, they spoke an archaic German language so they couldn't communicate with the external world, they didn't know where they were, they couldn't read a map that might allow them to escape, and they had no one to help them. This is not a unique case; the same has happened and still happens in other isolated fundamentalist communities, either religious or militant, such as Boko Haram, the Islamic terrorist organization in Nigeria, where women are treated like animals. Sometimes no ideology is needed, just isolation and ignorance, as in Tysfjord, in the north of Norway, near the Arctic.

Men fear feminine power. That's why

laws, religion, and strict mores have been imposed for centuries—all kinds of restrictions on women's intellectual, economic, and artistic development. In the past, thousands and thousands of women accused of witchery were tortured and burned alive because they knew too much; they had the power of knowledge. Women didn't have access to libraries or universities; in fact, the ideal was—and still is in some places—that women remain illiterate to keep them submissive and to stop them from questioning or rebelling. The same principle was applied to slaves. The punishment for learning to read was a whipping and even death. Today, most women have the same educational opportunities as men, but if they stand out or aspire to leadership positions they are met with aggression, as happened to Hillary Clinton in the 2016 U.S. presidential election.

———

MASS MURDERERS IN THE UNITED States—almost without exception, white men—have misogyny in common, along with a proven record of domestic violence, threats, and assaults on women. Many of these psychopaths have been marked by traumatic relationships with their mothers. They cannot stand rejection, indifference, or mockery from women; that is to say, they cannot stand the power that women have held over them. "Men are afraid that women will laugh at them. Women are afraid that men will kill them," wrote Margaret Atwood.

The Women's Liberation Movement has tested the self-esteem of two or three generations of men. They have been challenged and often surpassed by feminine competitiveness in many fields that used to belong to them exclusively, like the armed forces. The masculine response to women's empowerment is often violent. It's not a coincidence that there is a high rate of rape in the military, where in the past women could only work in administrative jobs, far from the action.

Of course, I am not saying that all men are potential abusers or rapists, but the percentage is so high that we have to consider violence against women for what it really is: the greatest crisis that faces humanity. The aggressors are not exceptional; they are fathers, brothers, boyfriends, husbands, and other normal men.

Enough of euphemisms. Enough of partial solutions. Profound changes are needed in society and it's us, women, who can impose them. Remember that no one gives us anything. We have to seize what we want. We need to create global awareness and get organized.

Now, more than ever before, this is possible because we have information, communication, and the ability to mobilize.

——

MISTREATMENT OF WOMEN CAN BE explained by how they are devalued. Feminism is the radical notion that, as Marie Shear said, women are people. For centuries it was debated whether or not women had souls. In many places a woman has less value than a cow or a horse. Most men consider women inferior, even if they would never admit it, so they are shocked and offended if a woman knows or achieves more than they do.

I have told this story before in a memoir, but I will summarize it here because it's relevant. Many years ago, in 1995, I traveled to India with Willie, my husband at the time, and my friend Tabra. The two of them planned the trip to push me out of my comfort zone and to help me shake the paralysis I felt after my daughter died. I had written a memoir—**Paula**—which helped me to understand and finally accept what had happened to her, but after it was published I found myself facing a terrible void. My life made no sense at all.

I remember the contrasts and the incredible beauty of India. I also remember something that influenced the rest of my life.

We had rented a car with a driver and were traveling on a rural road in Rajasthan when the engine overheated and we had to stop. While we waited for it to cool down, Tabra and I walked over to a group of six or seven women and some kids who were under the only tree in that place. What were they doing there in the desert? From where did they come? We had not passed any village or well that could explain their presence.

The women, all very young and poor, approached us with that innocent curiosity that still exists in some places. Tabra's hair, the color of eggplant, fascinated them. We gave them the silver bracelets that we had bought in a market and we played with the kids for a little while. Then the driver honked, calling us.

As we were leaving, one of the women came up to me and handed me a small parcel of rags. It weighed almost nothing. I thought she wanted to give me something in exchange for the bracelets, but when I opened the rags to see what was inside, I found a newborn baby. I blessed the baby and tried to give it back, but the mother stepped away and wouldn't take it. I was so surprised that I was unable to move, but the driver, a tall, bearded man in a turban, ran over, took the baby from me, and shoved it into another woman's hands. He grabbed me by the arm and dragged me to the car. We left in a hurry. Several minutes later, when I had recovered from the shock, I asked what had happened. Why had that woman tried to give me her baby? "It was a girl. No one wants a girl!" the driver answered.

Although I could not save that little girl, she has appeared in my dreams for years. I dream that she has had a miserable life, I dream that she died young, I dream that she is my daughter or my granddaughter. In her memory, I decided to create a foundation whose mission is to help other girls like her: girls nobody wants; girls who are sold into premature marriage, forced labor, and prostitution; girls who are beaten and raped; girls who give birth in puberty; girls who will be mothers of other girls like them in an eternal cycle of humiliation and suffering; millions of girls who die too soon and millions who don't even have the right to be born.

Now that fetus gender can be determined, millions of girls are aborted. In China, where the one-child-only policy to control population growth, implemented until 2016, caused a shortage of brides, many men import them from other countries, sometimes by force. It is estimated that twenty-one thousand girls were trafficked in less than five years from Myanmar (formerly Burma) to the Henan province, which has the highest disparity among the genders; one hundred and forty boys are born for every one hundred girls. Those trafficked girls, drugged, beaten, and raped, become captive wives and mothers, all against their will. One might think that given the demand, girls would be valued as much as boys, but that is not yet the case. In many places, it's considered a disgrace to have a daughter and a blessing to have a son. Midwives are even paid less if the newborn is a female.

—

ACCORDING TO THE WORLD HEALTH Organization, two hundred million women have suffered genital mutilation, and three million girls are at risk of suffering it right now in parts of Africa, Asia, and among some immigrant communities in Europe and the United States. If you can stomach it, please look this practice up online. The clitoris and labia of a girl's vulva are cut with a razor blade, knife, or piece of sharp glass, without anesthesia and with minimal hygiene. Women perform this mutilation on girls, repeating without question a custom that aims at preventing sexual pleasure and orgasm. Governments do not always intervene; it's considered a religious or cultural tradition, and a girl who has not been cut has less value in the matrimonial market.

Abuse, exploitation, and the torture of

women and girls happen on a massive scale throughout the world, usually with impunity. The figures are so high that they numb us and we lose perspective on the true horror. Only when we get to know a girl or a woman who has suffered these gruesome experiences—when we learn her name, see her face, and hear her story—can we stand in solidarity.

We suppose that nothing so terrible could happen to one of our daughters, but when they go out into the world and have to fend for themselves there will be innumerable instances in which they will be undervalued and harassed. At school and in higher education, girls are usually smarter and better students than boys, but they have fewer opportunities. In the workplace men still earn more and get the best promotions. In science and the arts women have to double their efforts for half the recognition . . . and so on.

Decades ago women were prevented from developing their talent and creativity because such development was considered an offense against nature; it was assumed that they were biologically predestined for motherhood only. If someone could achieve some degree of success, she had to hide behind her husband or father, who would get the credit, as was the case with composers, painters, writers, and scientists. That has changed, but not everywhere and not as much as is desirable.

In Silicon Valley, a technological paradise that has changed forever the essence of human communication and relationships, and where the average age is under thirty—that is to say, we are talking about a young generation that is supposedly the most progressive and visionary in the world—women still experience the same male-chauvinist discrimination that was unacceptable half a century ago. There, as in so many other places, the proportion of women employed is minimal; women are awarded fewer promotions, they are often harassed and undervalued, and interrupted or ignored when they speak.

My mother painted very well in oil—she had an exquisite sense of color—but because no one took her seriously, she didn't either. She grew up with the idea that because she was a woman she was limited; true artists and creators were men. I understand, because in spite of feminism I also doubted my ability and talent; I didn't start writing fiction until I was almost forty. I had the feeling I was trespassing into forbidden territory. Famous writers, especially those from the Latin American boom, were male. Panchita feared her creativity, as she explained it to me once. She preferred to copy other artists because it was not risky; no one was going to make fun of her or accuse her of being pretentious. She could have studied and put more effort into it, but nobody encouraged her. Her "little paintings" were considered yet another of her whims.

I always celebrated my mother's paintings. I brought them by the dozens to California, and today they cover the walls in my office and my home, including the garage. Panchita painted for me. I know she regretted not having prioritized her art, as eventually I was able to do with my writing.

———

LET'S TALK ABOUT PEACE. WAR IS THE maximum manifestation of machismo. In any war most of the victims are not combatants but women and children. Violence is the main cause of death among women fourteen to forty-four years of age, more than the sum of deaths due to cancer, malaria, and accidents. Seventy percent of human-trafficking victims are women and girls. It's fair to say that there is an undeclared war against women. No wonder we want peace above all, peace for us and for our children.

When I saw **The Vagina Monologues** by Eve Ensler, which is now a part of the culture everywhere, I was with my mother. We both left shaken to the core. At the end of the play Panchita said that she had never thought of her vagina, let alone looked at it in a mirror.

Eve Ensler wrote the **Monologues** in 1996 when the word **vagina** was considered rude and women barely dared mention it to their gynecologists. The play has been translated into many languages; it has been shown Off-Broadway, in schools and colleges, in the streets and plazas, and secretly in basements in those places where women lack fundamental rights. It has raised millions of dollars for programs dedicated to protecting and educating women and promoting their leadership.

Eve, who suffered sexual abuse at the hands of her own father, founded V-Day, a global initiative to end violence against women and girls. In Congo, V-Day built the City of Joy, a refuge for female victims of war, rape, kidnapping, abuse, incest, exploitation, torture, and genital mutilation, and for women who are in danger of being killed out of jealousy, revenge, or simply because they are collateral damage in armed conflicts. There they start to heal and regain their voices, to sing and dance and tell their stories. They learn to trust themselves and other women. They recover their souls. All return to the world transformed.

For decades Eve Ensler has witnessed

atrocities, but she has never wavered; she is sure that we can end this type of violence in one generation.

———

RAPE HAS BECOME A WEAPON OF WAR. Women are the primary victims of military invasion and occupation, paramilitary groups, guerrillas, and militant movements of any type, including religious and of course terrorist groups and gangs, like the redoubtable Central American **maras.** Up to a million girls and women have been raped in the last few years in Congo alone, from toddlers to great-grandmothers. They have been mutilated and disfigured, and many suffer fistulas so severe that they often cannot be repaired.

Rape destroys the bodies and lives of women and girls and the fabric of communities. The damage is so great that now men are being raped too. In this way militias and armies break the will and the soul of a civilian population. Victims suffer horrible physical and psychological traumas and are marked as tainted forever; often they are expelled from their families and villages or stoned to death. This is yet another instance in which the victim is blamed.

Kavita Ramdas, the former chief executive officer of the Global Fund for Women, the largest nonprofit dedicated to women's rights, and now the director of the Women's Rights Program at the Open Society Foundations, proposes demilitarizing the world. This goal can only be achieved by women, because we are not seduced by the male attraction to weapons and we are the ones who most suffer the impact of a culture that exalts violence.

There's nothing as fearsome as violence with impunity, as always happens in times of war. One of our most ambitious dreams is to end all wars, but there are too many interests invested in the war industry. A critical number of people willing to make this dream come true are needed to tip the balance toward peace.

Imagine a world without armies, a world where the resources employed in war are used for the common well-being, conflicts are resolved around a negotiation table, and the mission of soldiers is to maintain order and promote peace. When that happens we will exceed our condition as Homo sapiens, as we call the descendants of primates who can use a computer, and we will take an evolutionary leap toward **contentus homo superior.**

———

THERE'S NO FEMINISM WITHOUT ECONOMIC independence. I saw this very clearly in my childhood because of my mother's situation. Women need to have their own income and to manage it. To that end they need education, training, and an adequate work and family environment. That's not always the case.

A Samburu guide in Kenya told me that his father was looking for a bride for him who would be a good mother to his children, take care of his livestock, and perform domestic chores. In the future, she would probably ask him to find other wives who could help with her work. He explained that if she had other options, the fabric of the family and the community would fray. I understand this guide's reasons for wanting to preserve a tradition that's very convenient for him, but I would have liked to talk to that hypothetical bride and the village wives. Maybe they were not so happy with their fate, and if they had the education denied to them, they would aspire to a different life.

In 2015 it was estimated that two-thirds

of illiterate people in the world are women. Most children without schooling are girls. Women are paid less than men for the same job; occupations that traditionally belong to women, like teaching, caregiving, etc., are poorly paid; and housework is neither valued nor compensated. This is even more irritating nowadays, when women work outside the home to help support a family, and at the end of the day women go home, tired, to take care of children, cook, and clean. We have to change customs and laws.

We live in an unbalanced world. In some places women enjoy self-determination, at least in theory, while in others they are subject to men's demands, desires, and whims. In some regions women can't go out of the house without a male relative for company; they have no voice, no power to decide their destinies or those of their children, no education or proper healthcare, and no income; they don't participate in public life; they can't even decide when and whom they will marry.

By the middle of 2019, we saw in the press the good news that women in Saudi Arabia were finally permitted to drive cars and travel without a male relative. This was achieved after several women from the royal family escaped the kingdom and asked for asylum in foreign countries; they could no longer stand the repression in their nation. However, now that driving and traveling are legally allowed, they have to face anger from the men in their families who don't agree with the changes. This, in the twenty-first century!

When I say that I was a feminist at five—and proud to be one—it's not because I remember it; my mother has told me that it happened on an emotional level, before I could reason. Even then Panchita was worried about her strange daughter. When I was a girl in my grandfather's house, the men in the family had money, cars, and freedom to come and go anytime they wanted, as well as the authority to make all decisions, even the smallest ones, such as what would appear on the dinner menu. My mother had none of that; she lived off her father's and older brother's charity. She also had to protect her reputation. How much of that did I perceive? Enough to suffer for it.

Dependency was as horrifying to me in childhood as it is today; that's why by the time I graduated from high school, I planned to work to support myself and help my mother. My grandfather said that whoever pays gives the orders. That was the first axiom I incorporated into my budding feminism.

———

I WILL MENTION MY FOUNDATION briefly because it's related to all these issues. (You can look up the work we do at isabelallendefoundation.org.)

My memoir **Paula** was published in 1994 to an extraordinary response from readers. Every day, the mail brought letters in many languages from people who felt touched by my daughter's story. They identified with my bereavement because everybody experiences loss and pain. I had a mountain of mail in crates, some of the letters so beautiful that a couple of years later several European editors published a selection of them.

The income from the book belonged to my daughter, not to me. I deposited it in a separate account while I figured out what Paula would do with it. I made a decision after that memorable trip to India and created a foundation whose mission is to invest in the power of vulnerable women and girls. That was Paula's mission during her short life. It was a good decision because thanks to the foundation—which receives a substantial percentage of my income—my daughter is still in the world helping others. You can imagine what this means to me.

I don't need to invent the protagonists of my books, those strong and determined women, because I am surrounded by the likes of them. Some have escaped death and suffered terrible trauma; they have lost everything, including their children, and yet they survive. Even more, they rise, and some of them become leaders in their communities. They are proud of the scars on their bodies and the wounds of their souls because those scars and wounds prove their resilience. These women refuse to be treated as victims. They have dignity and courage, they get up and go forward without losing their capacity for love, compassion, and joy. With a little empathy and solidarity they recover and thrive.

Sometimes I am disheartened. I ask myself whether my foundation's contribution is but a drop of water in a desert of need. There's so much to do and our resources are so limited! This is a pernicious doubt because it invites us to wash our hands of the suffering of others. In those moments, Lori, my daughter-in-law, who runs the foundation, reminds me that our impact cannot be measured on a universal scale, it has to be measured case by case. We can't shrug at problems that seem insurmountable, we have to act. Lori reminds me of those selfless and courageous people who work in very difficult conditions with no other goal than to meet the needs and alleviate the suffering of others. With their example, they force us to exorcise the demon of indifference.

———

MY FOUNDATION FOCUSES ON HEALTH (including reproductive rights), education, economic independence, and protection against violence and exploitation. Since 2016 it has also worked with refugees, especially along the southern border of the United States, where there's a humanitarian crisis in the form of thousands and thousands of people who have escaped violence in Central America and seek asylum. Women and children suffer the greatest risks. Restrictive measures by the U.S. government have practically eliminated the rights of asylum seekers.

The argument against migrants is that they burden social services, they take away jobs, and they change the culture, a euphemism to indicate that they are not white. However, it's a proven fact that when allowed to integrate into the country, immigrants contribute much more than they take.

There's a difference between immigrants and refugees. The former decide to move somewhere else to improve their lives. They are usually young and healthy (the elderly stay behind), they try to adapt as soon as possible, they look to the future, and they want to plant roots in the new place. The latter are running for their lives; they are escaping military conflict, persecution, crime, and extreme poverty. Refugees are desperate, they have had to leave behind everything that is familiar to them and seek asylum in another country where they are likely to confront hostility. Half of the seventy million refugees in 2018 were women and children, a figure that has been increasing yearly.

Refugees live on memories and nostalgia; they have their eyes in the past and they dream of going back home, but the average time they will spend away is between seventeen and twenty-five years. Most will never return; they will always be foreigners. This global crisis, which will be aggravated by new waves of refugees forced to leave their land due to climate change, cannot be solved by building walls. It's necessary to confront the causes that force people to flee their places of origin.

———

You have to understand,
that no one puts their children in
  a boat
unless the water is safer than
  the land
no one burns their palms
under trains
beneath carriages
no one spends days and nights in
  the stomach of a truck
feeding on newspaper unless the
  miles travelled
means something more
  than journey.
no one crawls under fences

no one wants to be beaten
pitied

no one chooses refugee camps
or strip searches where your
body is left aching
or prison,
because prison is safer
than a city on fire
and one prison guard
in the night
is better than a truckload
of men who look like your father

—"HOME" BY WARSAN SHIRE

—

ONE OF THE MOST EFFICIENT WAYS TO have a positive impact in the world is by investing in women. In less developed regions, mothers typically spend their income on the family, while men spend only one-third of it on the family. Women spend on food, healthcare, and schooling for their children, while men spend on themselves, either for entertainment or for something that gives them status, like a cellphone or a bike.

I have learned that with a little help a lot can be achieved. If a woman can make decisions for herself and has some income, the situation in the family improves. If families prosper, the community and, eventually, the country prosper. Thus, the cycle of poverty is broken. The least developed societies are those in which women are submissive. However, this obvious truth is often ignored by both governments and nongovernmental organizations (NGOs). Fortunately, this is changing as more women gain political power and resources for philanthropy, which they generally dedicate to women's projects.

———

WOMEN NEED TO BE CONNECTED TO ONE another. According to Adrienne Rich, an American feminist and poet, connections among women are the most feared and potentially most transforming force on the planet. This interesting observation could explain why men are so uncomfortable when women get together. They think we are colluding, and sometimes they are right.

Since the beginning of time women have gathered at the well, the kitchen, the cradle, and in fields, factories, and homes. They want to share their lives and hear others' stories. There's nothing as entertaining as women's talk, which is almost always intimate and personal. Gossiping is also fun, no point in denying that. Our nightmare is to be excluded and isolated because alone we are vulnerable while together we thrive. However, millions of women live confined, without the freedom or means to move beyond the limited radius of their homes.

A few years ago, Lori and I visited a small women's community in Kenya. We had been given rather vague directions, but Lori, who is much more adventurous than I, ordered me to put on a hat and start walking along a trail that snaked through the vegetation. Soon the trail disappeared and we continued blindly for a while. I had the feeling we would be lost forever, but Lori's motto is that "all roads lead to Rome." Finally, when I was on the verge of tears, we heard voices. It was an undulating chant of female voices, like waves along the seashore. That was the compass that guided us to Kibisom.

We arrived at a clearing in the thicket, a large patio with a couple of basic dwellings and something like a barn for cooking, eating, sewing, classes, and crafts. We had come to see Esther Odhiambo, a professional woman who retired after years of work in Nairobi and decided to return to her village near Lake Victoria. There she discovered a real tragedy. Men came and went in a nomadic existence as they looked for work, there was no economic stability, prostitution was rampant, and AIDS had decimated the population, killing a generation of mothers and fathers; only grandparents and children remained. Women died at the same rate as men.

When Esther arrived there was very little information about the illness and how it was transmitted—the villagers believed it was caused by black magic—and there was no treatment available. She was determined to confront superstition, educate people, and help women, in particular, with her few resources, which included her house.

Upon our arrival, Lori and I saw children playing, while others did schoolwork, writing with chalk on small slates or drawing numbers and letters with a stick on the ground. Groups of women were cooking, doing laundry, or working at their crafts, which they sold in the market to help support the community.

We introduced ourselves in English and Esther translated. Seeing that we were foreigners and that we had come from afar, the women gathered around us, offering a bitter red tea. Then they sat in a circle to tell us about their lives, which consisted mainly of work, loss, pain, and love.

They were widows, abandoned wives, pregnant teenagers, grandmothers in charge of orphaned grandchildren or great-grandchildren. There was also a woman who seemed very old, although she didn't know her age, who was breast-feeding an infant. Seeing our astonishment, Esther explained to us that it sometimes happens that a grandmother is able to produce milk again because she has to feed a baby. "This lady must be around eighty years old," she added, though maybe she exaggerated. I have told this story many times and nobody around here believes me, but I saw something similar in a small village in Lake Atitlán, in Guatemala.

The stories of the Kibisom women were tragic; some of them had lost almost every member of their families to AIDS, but they didn't seem sad. In that circle any excuse was good enough to laugh, to joke, to tease one another, and to make fun of Lori and me. Esther summarized it in one sentence: "When women are together, they get happy." In the late afternoon they said goodbye to us, singing. Those ladies sang all the time.

It's possible that the small community of Kibisom no longer exists, because this adventure with Lori happened several years ago, but I have never forgotten its lessons. I can easily visualize groups of women like those at Kibisom, women of all races, creeds, and ages, sitting in circles sharing their stories, their struggles and their hopes, crying, laughing, and working together. What a powerful force those circles would create! Millions of connected circles could end the patriarchy. It wouldn't be bad, would it? We have to give feminine energy—an immense, renewable, and natural resource—a chance.

———

IN THE 1960S, WHEN THE BIRTH CONTROL pill and other contraceptives became available, women's liberation expanded because finally women could exert control over their bodies and enjoy a satisfactory sexual life without the terror of an unwanted pregnancy. Imagine the opposition of the Catholic Church and Chilean machismo! I assumed then that the end of the patriarchy was inevitable, but we are still far from seeing that happen. We have obtained much, but we still have much to do. Any excuse is good enough to squash our rights, when we have them: war, fundamentalism, dictatorship, economic crisis, catastrophe, etc. In the United States of the twenty-first century, not only is abortion under scrutiny but also female contraception. Of course nobody discusses a man's right to a vasectomy or condoms.

My foundation helps finance fertility control clinics and programs, including abortion. This issue is close to my heart because at eighteen I had to help a fifteen-year-old high school student who got pregnant. I will call her Celina because I can't mention her real name. She came to me because she didn't dare tell her parents. In her despair she contemplated suicide; that's how terrible the stigma was then. In Chile abortion was severely punished by law but was widely practiced clandestinely, and still is. Conditions were then, and are today, very dangerous.

I don't remember how I got the name of someone who could solve Celina's problem. We took two buses to reach a modest neighborhood and then walked around for half an hour looking for the address I had written on a piece of paper. Finally, we got to an apartment on the third floor of a brick building similar to a dozen others on the same street. Clothes hung from wires on windows and over-flowing garbage cans lined the entrance. A tired-looking woman was waiting for us because I had called her on the phone and given her the name of the person who had referred us. She screamed at a couple of kids who were playing in the living room to go to their room. Obviously the children knew the routine because they left without complaining.

In the kitchen a radio blasted the news and commercials.

The woman asked Celina the date of her last menstruation, made her calculations, and seemed satisfied. She told us she was quick and safe, and for a little more than the original price she would use anesthesia. She placed a plastic tablecloth on the only table in the place, probably the dining table, and ordered Celina to take off her underwear and lie down. She examined her briefly and then placed an IV line in her arm. "I was a nurse, I have experience," she explained. She added that my job was to inject just enough anesthetic to stun my friend. "Careful, not too much," she warned me.

In a few seconds Celina was semi-conscious and in less than fifteen minutes there were several bloody rags in a bucket on the floor. I didn't want to imagine what that intervention would have been like without anesthesia, as is usually the case in those circumstances. My hands trembled so much that I don't know how I managed with the syringe. When it was over, I asked for the bathroom and vomited.

Minutes later, when Celina woke up, the woman dismissed us without giving her time to recover. She handed Celina a few pills. "Antibiotics. Take one every twelve hours for three days. If you get a fever or start bleeding too much, you will have to go to the hospital, but that's not going to happen. I am good at this," she said. She warned us that if we gave anyone her name or address, the consequences for us would be dire.

—

THIS EXPERIENCE HAPPENED ALMOST sixty years ago and I have not been able to forget it. I have described it in several of my books and I relive it in my nightmares. For Celina and the millions of women who have suffered something similar, I am inflexible in defending reproductive rights. If abortion is legal and practiced under appropriate conditions, it does not have to be as traumatic an experience, as many studies have shown. Women who are not able to get an abortion and are forced to carry an unwanted pregnancy to term suffer more trauma.

I respect people who reject abortion for religious or other reasons, but it is not acceptable that they impose their view on those who do not share it. Abortion should be an option available to those who need it.

Contraception should be free and available to girls once they start menstruating. If that were the case, there would be fewer unwanted pregnancies. In reality, contraception is expensive, often requires a prescription, is not always covered by insurance, and can have disagreeable side effects. Also, there's no guarantee that it will always work.

The burden of family planning is on the woman. Many men refuse to use condoms and ejaculate without thinking of the consequences. Women and girls end up being blamed for not having been careful enough. There's a saying in Spanish: **Se dejó preñar,** which means that she allowed herself to get pregnant, and implies that she should pay for it. Those who oppose abortion don't place any responsibility on the man, without whom fertilization is not possible. Neither do they ask about the practical or emotional reasons behind a woman's choice to end a pregnancy, or what a child would mean for her at that stage of her life.

I have been lucky; I never went through anything like what Celina endured. I could plan my family—two children—first with the pill and then with an IUD.

However, in my late thirties I could no longer tolerate any of the usual contraceptive methods and ended up having a tubal ligation. I thought that decision was my only option but I resented it for a long time afterward, partly because the surgery was complicated and I developed a serious infection, and partly because I felt mutilated. Why did I have to go through that? Why didn't my husband get a vasectomy instead? It's a much simpler procedure. Well, because despite my feminism, I didn't demand it.

Both my granddaughters have decided that they are not going to have children because it's too much work and the planet is overpopulated. On the one hand it saddens me a little that they will miss out on that experience, which was wonderful for me, but on the other hand I am happy that these young women have that option. I am afraid, however, that our family will be extinguished unless my only grandson steps up and finds a willing partner.

—

WOMEN WERE ABLE TO CONTROL THEIR fertility for centuries. They had knowledge of the menstrual cycle and of herbs and abortive methods, but that knowledge was brutally rooted out. As a consequence of the devaluation of women, men arrogated for themselves dominion over the female body.

Who makes decisions about a woman's body and the number of children she can have? Men in politics, religion, and law who don't experience pregnancy, childbirth, or motherhood. Unless laws, religion, and culture place the same responsibility for a pregnancy on the father as the mother, men should not be allowed to have an opinion in this matter. It's none of their business. This is a personal decision for each woman. Control over one's fertility is a human right.

In Nazi Germany abortion was punished with prison for the woman, and death for the practitioner. Women had to produce children for the nation. The mothers of eight or more children were awarded a gold medal. In several Latin American countries, laws about this are so draconian that a miscarriage is immediately deemed suspicious and the woman may be accused of having induced it and end up in prison for years. In Chile in 2013, a girl called Belen, eleven years old, was raped by her stepfather and got pregnant. She was not allowed to have an abortion despite the campaigns of several civil organizations and an international scandal.

Abortion should be decriminalized; that is, it should not be punished. That's different from legalizing it, because the laws are imposed by the patriarchy and power stays in the hands of judges, the police, politicians, and other male institutions. As an aside, this is the same reason sex workers aren't asking for prostitution to be legalized, but rather for it to be decriminalized.

Steve King, a congressman from the United States, proposed abolishing the right to abortion even in the case of rape or incest. "What if we went back through all the family trees and just pulled those people out that were products of rape and incest? Would there be any population of the world left if we did that? Considering all the wars and all the rape and pillage that's taken place . . . I know that I can't certify that I'm not a part of a product of that." In summary, a defense of rape and incest as natural and normal. Eighty-four congressmen from the Republican Party signed this proposal.

A former American congressman,

Todd Akin, said that rape rarely resulted in a pregnancy. "If it's legitimate rape [?], the female body has ways to try to shut the whole thing down." So, according to him, the uterus magically knows when it's "legitimate rape" versus other forms of sex. This genius was a member of the House of Representatives Committee on Science, Space and Technology.

In the United States, there are thirty-two thousand reported cases of pregnancy resulting from rape annually.

———

WOMEN NEED TO HAVE CONTROL OVER their lives as much as they need to control their fertility, but none of that is possible if they suffer domestic violence and their fate is in the hands of an abuser.

Years ago, in the late 1960s and early 1970s, when I worked as a journalist in Chile, I reported more than once on very poor neighborhoods. Families there lived in shacks made of cardboard and wooden planks, the men were jobless, often alcoholic, and the women were burdened with many children and were victims of poverty, abuse, and exploitation. A common scenario would be that a man would come home drunk or simply frustrated and beat up his wife or children. The police didn't intervene, partly due to indifference and because they sometimes did the same in their homes, and partly because supposedly they could not enter the dwelling without a warrant. Faced with this reality, when women neighbors heard a wife or kids screaming they would break in, armed with pots and pans, and give the aggressor what he deserved. Their method was quick and efficient.

I am ashamed to admit that Chile was then, and continues to be, one of the countries with the highest rates of domestic violence in the world. It's possible that more cases are reported than in other places, and that the statistics are more accurate. It happens in every social stratum, but in the upper classes it's kept hidden. Sometimes there's no physical abuse but there is psychological mistreatment, and emotional torture can be just as harmful.

One in three women suffer some kind of physical or sexual abuse in their lives regardless of their appearance or their age. This brings to mind a song composed by four young Chilean women in 2019, which went viral globally. It became a feminist hymn and has been translated into many languages and played in streets and other public venues by thousands and thousands of blindfolded women. The song summarizes in a few lines what every woman experiences or fears.

And the fault wasn't mine,
Not where I went or how I
    was dressed.
The rapist was you.
The rapist was you.

—"A RAPIST IN YOUR PATH"
            BY LAS TESIS

The Chilean police, well known for their aggressive methods, have filed a lawsuit against Las Tesis for "threats to the institution, attacks on authority, and inciting hatred and violence."

———

VIOLENCE AGAINST WOMEN HAS BEEN SO common for millennia that we all avoid risky situations automatically. That limits us very much. What most men do without a second thought, like walking at night on the street, going into a bar, or hitchhiking, turns on an alarm in us. Is it worth the risk?

Domestic violence is so prevalent that Chile's first female president, Michelle Bachelet (who served from 2006 to 2010, and again from 2014 to 2018), prioritized in her administration the battle against violence in the family. She implemented education, training, information, shelters, and protective laws. She also provided free and easy access to contraception, but she couldn't get Congress to decriminalize abortion.

The life of this feminist hero is like a novel. She studied medicine as a way to help people in need, she said in an interview, and specialized in pediatrics. Her father, General Alberto Bachelet, was killed by the military dictatorship. He was arrested by his comrades in arms because he refused to join them in the uprising against the democratic government;

he subsequently died of a heart attack while being tortured.

Michelle and her mother were also arrested by the secret police and tortured in the infamous Villa Grimaldi, which is now a museum of the atrocities committed during those years. When Michelle was rescued, she went into exile in Australia, and later to East Germany. Years later, she returned to Chile, where she was able to finish her medical training and then worked in different positions until the reinstatement of democracy in 1990, when she started her political career.

As minister of health she authorized the distribution of the morning-after pill, to avoid pregnancy immediately after sex, to women and girls over fourteen years old. In Chile, where the Catholic Church and the right-wing parties are very powerful, this measure created tremendous opposition but also won her respect and popularity.

In 2017 the Chilean Congress approved abortion in three instances: threat to the life of the mother, inviability of the fetus outside the womb, and rape. In cases of rape, it had to be done within the first twelve weeks of gestation, or by fourteen weeks if the girl was fourteen or younger. The restrictions even in these cases, however, are such that the law is almost a mockery destined to placate the majority of women who demand it. During the mass demonstrations that this law generated, many women marched topless to emphasize that they own their own bodies.

In 2002 Michelle was appointed minister of national defense, making her the first woman to hold that position in Latin America and one of the few in the world. She had the Herculean task of trying to reconcile the military and the victims of the dictatorship, and to obtain from the armed forces the promise that they would never again overturn democracy.

I can't even imagine how this woman could overcome the trauma of the past and deal with the institution that imposed a regime of terror for seventeen years upon her country, assassinated her father, tortured her and her mother, and forced her into exile. One of her torturers lived in her same building and they would occasionally meet in the elevator.

When asked about the need for national reconciliation Michelle replied that it was a personal decision. No one can demand forgiveness of the victims of repression. The country has to go forward into the future with the heavy burden of the past.

———

**I will walk the streets again
Of what once was
bloody Santiago**

**And in a beautiful
liberated square
Will pause to weep for those who
are absent**

—"I WILL WALK THE STREETS
AGAIN" BY PABLO MILANÉS

—

THE CALIPH OF BAGHDAD WOULD HAVE
liked to know that women want love
above all. We have something weird in
our brains, a sort of tumor that propels
us toward love. We can't live without it.
Out of love we put up with children and
men. Our self-denial is a form of servitude. Have you noticed that individual-
ism and selfishness are considered positive
traits in men and defects in women? We
tend to postpone fulfilling our needs in
favor of our children, our partners, our
parents, and almost everyone else. We

submit and make sacrifices for love—
that seems to us the height of nobility.
The more we suffer for love, the nobler
we are, as is clearly expressed in soap op-
eras. Culture exalts love as the most sublime sentiment, and we fall willingly into
that delicious trap due to the tumor in
our brains. I include myself: My tumor
is one of the most malign.

I will not talk about maternal love because it is untouchable and for any joke
I dare make about it I will have to pay a
high price. Once I told my son, Nicolás,
that instead of bringing children into
the world he could get a dog, and he has
never forgiven me. He married at twenty-
two and had three children in five years.
His maternal instinct is overdeveloped.
As for me, my grandchildren are okay,
but I also love dogs.

I can't criticize mothers' obsessive love
because that's probably the only reason
why species have survived, from bats

to technocrats. Nor will I refer to the love of nature, gods, goddesses, or other similar concepts because this is not even close to a scholarly lecture, it's just an informal chat.

Let's talk instead about romantic love, that collective illusion that has become yet another product of consumerism. The romance industry competes with narco trafficking in creating addiction. I suppose romance has a different meaning for each woman. Not all are obsessed with a movie actor, like myself, and there must be those who fall in love with a frog, like the princess in the fairy tale. In my case the physical attributes of the chosen one are irrelevant so long as he smells good, has his own teeth, and doesn't smoke. However, I have other requirements that are rarely found together in real life: tenderness, a sense of humor, the patience to put up with me, and other qualities that I can't remember

right now. Fortunately, my current beloved has them in abundance.

———

IT'S TIME TO TALK ABOUT ROGER, AS
promised.

The unforgettable lessons of my grandfather's rigorous school were very useful.
They forged my character and helped
me overcome moments of great adver-
sity, but they had a negative influence on
my love relationships. I don't surrender; I
am self-sufficient and very independent;
it's very easy for me to give and very difficult to receive. I don't accept favors unless I can give back; I hate to get presents
and don't allow anybody to celebrate my
birthday. One of my greatest challenges
was to accept my vulnerability, but now
it's much easier thanks to a new love,
which hopefully will be the last one.

One day in May 2016, a widowed
lawyer from New York named Roger heard

me on the radio while he was driving from Manhattan to Boston. He had read a couple of my books, and something that I said must have captured his attention because he wrote to my office. I answered, and he kept on writing every morning and every evening for five months. I usually answer only the first message from a reader because it would be impossible to have a correspondence with the hundreds of people who write to me, but the New York widower's tenacity impressed me. We kept in touch.

My assistant at the time, Chandra, who is addicted to detective TV series and has the nose of a bloodhound, decided to find out as much as possible about the mysterious widower. He could have been a psychopath; one never knows. You wouldn't believe how much information is available to anyone who wants to dig into someone's private life. Suffice it to say that Chandra handed me a large file, which included even the man's license plate number and the names of his five grandchildren. His wife had died a few years before; he lived alone in a large house in Scarsdale, New York; he took the train to Manhattan daily; his office was on Park Avenue; etc. "He seems legit, but we can't trust anybody; he could be an accomplice of Brenda's architect," Chandra warned me.

In October I traveled to New York to a conference and Roger and I finally met. I ascertained that he was exactly the guy I had seen in his emails and whom Chandra had investigated: transparent. I liked him but it wasn't the lightning bolt of sudden passion, as had happened with Willie when I was forty-five. This confirms what I said before about passion: Hormones matter a lot. Roger invited me to dinner, and a half hour into the meal I asked him point-blank what his intentions were. "I am seventy-four and

I don't have time to waste," I explained. He choked on his ravioli but did not try to run, as I would have done if he had ambushed me that way.

We were together for three days and then I had to return home. That time was enough for Roger to decide that now that he had found me, he was not going to let me go. He asked me to marry him on the way to the airport. I answered as any respectable mature lady would: "Marriage is out of the question, but if you are willing to travel frequently to California we can be lovers. What do you think?" Poor man . . . what could he answer? Yes, of course.

That's what we did for several months until the effort of meeting for just a weekend after a whole day of traveling became too much. Roger sold his old house, which was filled with furniture, objects, and memories; he gave away everything it contained and moved to

California with two bikes and his clothes, which I promptly replaced because they were dated. "I have nothing left. If this doesn't work, I will be homeless under a bridge," he said, worried.

———

FOR A YEAR AND SEVEN MONTHS WE tested our relationship, living together in my dollhouse with two dogs. We both had to compromise. I have to tolerate his mess and he my bossy temperament, my extreme punctuality, and my writing obsession, which doesn't leave me much free time for other endeavors. We learned the delicate dance of couples who get along and can move on the dance floor without stepping on each other's toes. Once we were sure that we could stand each other, we got married, because he is a traditional sort of guy and the idea of living in sin worried him. It was an intimate wedding, held in the company of our children and grandchildren only. They are all delighted by our marriage because it means that they will not have to take care of us just yet; Roger and I will take care of each other for as long as we can.

My mother would also be happy for us. A few days before she died, she told me to marry Roger because she didn't want me to be old and alone. I explained that I didn't feel old or alone. "If I have a perfect lover waiting for me in California, why would I want an imperfect husband?" I argued. "Lovers don't last; a husband is a captive prey," she replied.

———

I AM A BIT EMBARRASSED TO ADMIT THAT I depend on this lover/husband for several tasks that before I could perform easily, like filling the gas tank of the car and changing lightbulbs. Roger was born and raised in the Bronx, the product of Polish parents; he has heavy peasant hands and a mellow character. He helps me deal with this world's inconveniences without making me feel like a moron. I am glad I listened to my mother when she said I should marry him. He is a good captive prey; hopefully he won't change.

My son asked Roger what he felt when he met me and, blushing, he answered: "I felt like a teenager. And now I feel like a kid who wakes up every day knowing that he is going to the circus." Everything is relative. This is the most peaceful time in my life; there's no melodrama. Roger, on the other hand, thinks the daily excitement around me never ends; there's no time to get bored. Maybe he misses some tedium.

And what did I feel when I met him? Curiosity and a certain flutter in my stomach that before could lead me to reckless action and now warns me to go slowly and carefully. But I don't listen. My theory and practice is to say yes to life and then I'll see how I manage along the way.

In summary, if I found a sweetheart, there's hope for any old woman who wants a companion.

—

**Returning to seventeen
after having lived through
   a century
is like deciphering signs
without benefit of wisdom
to be suddenly once again
as fragile as one second
to feel things as intensely
as a child in front of God,
that's what it is like for me
in this very fertile instant.**

—"RETURNING TO SEVENTEEN"
BY VIOLETA PARRA

—

YOUNG PEOPLE ASK ME OFTEN HOW IS it to love at my age. They are amazed that I can still speak in full sentences, let alone fall in love. Well, it's the same as falling in love at seventeen, as Violeta Parra wrote, but with a greater sense of urgency. Roger and I have only a few years ahead of us. Years sneak by quickly, on tiptoe, scoffing, and suddenly they give us a fright in the mirror or smack us on the back. Every minute is precious and we can't waste it on misunderstanding, impatience, jealousy, pettiness, or the other silly stuff that soils relationships. In truth this formula can be applied at any age because it's always the case that our days are limited. If I had lived this way before, maybe I would not have two divorces behind me.

—

ACCORDING TO REBECCA SOLNIT IN HER book **Men Explain Things to Me,** "Feminism is an endeavor to change something very old, widespread, and deeply rooted in many, perhaps most, cultures around the world, innumerable institutions, and most households on earth—and in our minds where it all begins and ends. That so much change has been made in four or five decades is amazing; that everything is not permanently, definitively, irrevocably changed is not a sign of failure."

To dismantle the system that sustains civilization is very difficult and takes time, but we are achieving it bit by bit. The complex and fascinating task of inventing a new order to replace it is long. We advance two steps forward and fall one step back, stumbling, falling, getting back up, making mistakes, and celebrating ephemeral victories. There are moments of terrible disenchantment and others of great impetus, as has been the case with the #MeToo movement and the massive women's marches in many cities around the world. Nothing can stop us if we share a vision of the future and we are determined to make it come true together.

Patriarchy has not always existed. It is not inherent to the human condition, it is imposed by culture. We have kept a record of our presence on the planet since the invention of writing, around five thousand years ago in Mesopotamia; that's nothing compared to the more or less two hundred thousand years of Homo sapiens' existence. History is written by men and they exalt or omit facts according to their convenience. The feminine half of humanity is ignored in official history.

Who challenged machismo before the Women's Liberation Movement? Racism, colonization, exploitation, property, distribution of income, and other manifestations of the patriarchy were questioned, but women were not included in those analyses. It was assumed that gender division was a biological or divine imperative, and that power naturally fell to men. But it was not always that way. Before male dominance there were other forms of organization. Let's try to remember them or imagine them.

———

IT'S POSSIBLE THAT I WILL SEE PROFOUND change on more fronts before I die because young people are as anxious as we are; they are our allies. They are in a hurry. They are fed up with the economic model, the systematic destruction of nature, corrupt governments, discrimination, and the inequality that separates us and creates violence. They feel that the world they will inherit and have to manage is a disaster. The vision of a better world is shared by activists, artists, scientists, ecologists, various spiritual groups unconnected to any form of organized religion—which almost without exception are reactionary and patriarchal institutions—and many others. We have a lot of work to do, my friends. We have to clean house.

First of all, we need to end the patriarchy, an ancient institution that exalts masculine values (and flaws) and represses the female half of humanity. We have to question everything, from religion and laws to science and cultural mores. We are going to get really angry, so angry that our fury will smash the foundations that support this civilization. Docility, praised as a feminine virtue, is our worst enemy; it has never served us well, it is only convenient for men.

Respect, compliance, and fear, which are instilled in women from infancy, are so detrimental to us that we don't even know our own power. So great is that power, the patriarchy's goal is to crush it by any means, including the worst forms of violence. These methods are so successful that frequently the most rabid defenders of the patriarchy are women.

The activist Mona Eltahawy, who starts all her speeches with the statement "Fuck the patriarchy!" says that we have to defy, disobey, and disrupt. There's no other way. There are more than enough reasons to fear confrontation, as shown by the dreadful statistics of women sold, beaten, raped, tortured, and killed with impunity all over the world, not to mention other less lethal ways of silencing and scaring us. **Defy, disobey,** and **disrupt** is for young women who don't have the responsibility of motherhood, and for grandmothers who are past their reproductive years.

It's time that women participate in the management of this pathetic world on terms equal to men. Often women in power behave like hard men because it's been the only way they could compete and command, but when we reach a critical number of women in positions of power and leadership we will tip the balance toward a more just and egalitarian civilization.

More than forty years ago Bella Abzug, the famous activist and congresswoman from New York, summarized the above in one sentence: "In the twenty-first century women will change the nature of power instead of power changing the nature of women."

———

MY DAUGHTER MUST HAVE BEEN AROUND twenty years old when she suggested that

I shouldn't talk so much about feminism because it was dated and not sexy. We were already feeling the backlash against women's lib, which had achieved so much. Paula and I had a monumental argument. I explained to her that feminism, like all revolutions, is an organic phenomenon subject to change and revision.

Paula belonged to a generation of privileged young women who benefited from the struggles of their mothers and grandmothers and then rested on those laurels, thinking that everything was done. I explained to her that the majority of women had not yet received those benefits, and that they were resigned to their fate. They thought, as my mother had assured me, that the world is like this and it can't be changed. "If for any reason you don't like the word **feminist,** look for another word. The name is not important as long as the work gets done for yourself and for your sisters in the rest of the world who need it," I told her. Paula answered with a sigh, rolling her eyes to the ceiling.

Men succeed in depicting feminists as hysterical and hairy bitches. No wonder young women in their reproductive years, as Paula was then, were scared by the term; it could chase away potential boyfriends. However, as soon as my daughter graduated from university and started working, she enthusiastically embraced the ideas she had heard about since childhood. She had a Sicilian boyfriend, a charming young man who was waiting for her to learn to cook pasta to get married and have six children. He approved of Paula's choice to study psychology because it would help her in raising children, but when she decided to specialize in human sexuality he broke up with her. He could not tolerate that his bride would go around measuring other men's penises and orgasms. I don't blame him; poor young man.

My daughter died a long time ago and I still think of her every single day when I wake up in the morning and when I go to bed at night. I miss her so much! She would have been very happy to see today's new wave of young feminists, who are defiant, creative, and have a sense of humor.

———

THIS IS A HAPPY TIME FOR ME. HAPPINESS is not exuberant or noisy like joy or pleasure, it is silent, calm, and soft; it is an internal feeling of well-being that starts with loving myself. I am free. I don't have to prove anything to anybody, nor do I have to care for my children or grandchildren. They are all self-sufficient adults. I have done my duty, as my grandfather would say, and I have done more than was expected of me.

Some people have plans for the future; they even think of a career, but as I said before, the only goal I've had since childhood was to support myself and I have done it. But I have walked the rest of my journey blindly. John Lennon said that life is what happens when we are busy making other plans. In other words, life is a mapless road and we can't go back. I had no control over the important events that determined my destiny or my personality, such as my father's disappearance, the military coup in Chile, exile, my daughter's death, the success of **The House of the Spirits,** or my two divorces. Of course, it could be argued that I had control over the divorces, but the success of a marriage depends on both participants.

My old age is a precious gift. My brain still works. I like my brain. I feel lighter. I am free of self-doubt, irrational desires, useless complexes, and other deadly sins that are not worth the trouble. I am letting go . . . letting go. I should have started earlier.

People come and go, and even the closest members of the family eventually disperse. It's useless to cling to anybody or anything because everything in the universe tends toward separation, chaos, and entropy, not cohesion. I have chosen a simpler life, with fewer material things and more leisure, fewer worries and more fun, fewer social commitments and more true friendship, less fuss and more silence.

I don't know if I would have achieved all of the above without the success of my books, which have saved me from the economic instability that affects a great majority of the elderly. I can enjoy freedom because I have the necessary resources to live the way I want. That's a privilege.

Every morning when I wake up, after

greeting Paula, Panchita, and other present spirits, when the room is still dark and silent, I call back my soul, which is still roaming in the land of dreams, and I give thanks for all I have, particularly for love, good health, and writing. And I also give thanks for the rich and passionate life I have and will continue to have. I am not ready to pass the torch and hopefully I never will be. I want to light the torches of our daughters and granddaughters with mine. They will have to live for us, as we lived for our mothers, and carry on with the work we didn't have time to finish.

———

I AM WRITING THIS IN MARCH 2020, forced by the coronavirus to remain locked at home with Roger. (Instead, I should be writing a novel inspired by García Márquez: **Love in the Time of Pandemic.**) At our age, if Roger or I caught the virus we would be screwed. We can't complain; we are a thousand times safer than the heroes of our time, women and men fighting the virus in the front lines, and much more comfortable than most people who now are forced to remain quarantined until further notice. It pains me to think of the elderly who are alone, to think of the sick, the homeless, those who survive with almost nothing and have no safety net or help, the families who live crowded in unhealthy tenements, those who survive in refugee camps, and so many others who are suffering this emergency without resources.

Roger and I are very lucky. The dogs provide entertainment and company; we are not bored. Roger works remotely from his computer, I write quietly in the attic, and in our spare time we read and watch movies on TV. We're still allowed to get out for a walk, as long as we keep a distance of six feet from other people;

that helps us clear our minds. Maybe this is the honeymoon that we never had because we were too busy. We have been in this strange retreat for a week and we are still doing well, but I am afraid that if this crisis goes on much longer we will run out of the patience, kindness, and discipline to put up with each other. Forced and close coexistence can be very irritating. I have heard that in China, where the quarantine was first imposed, hundreds of thousands of couples have filed for divorce.

No one alive remembers a global catastrophe of this magnitude. In extreme situations the best and the worst emerge in people; heroes and villains appear. Also, the character of a nation is manifested. In Italy people sing opera on their balconies to cheer one another; in other places people buy guns. And I was told that in Chile the sales of chocolate, wine, and condoms have increased!

We could not have imagined that in just a few days the known world would be so disrupted. All social life has been suspended, and all gatherings are forbidden, from football games to Alcoholics Anonymous meetings. Schools, universities, restaurants, coffee shops, bookstores, malls, and much more are closed. Traveling is out of the question. Those who have some savings are withdrawing them from the bank and hiding them under their mattresses. The stock market has plummeted. The moment of truth has finally come to our unsustainable consumer economy. The streets are empty, the cities are quiet, nations are scared, and many of us are questioning our civilization.

However, not all news is bad. Pollution has diminished, the water in the Venetian canals is clear, the sky in Beijing has turned blue, and birds are singing among the skyscrapers of New York. Relatives, friends, colleagues, and neighbors communicate as much as they can to give one another support. Lovers previously undecided now plan to move in together as soon as they can reunite. Suddenly we realized that what really matters is love.

Pessimists say that this is a dystopian science fiction nightmare, and that human beings divided into savage tribes will end up devouring one another, like in Cormac McCarthy's terrifying novel **The Road.** Realists think that this will pass, as so many other catastrophes have passed throughout history, and we will have to deal with the long-term consequences. We, the optimists, believe that this is the shock needed to amend our course, a unique opportunity to make profound changes. We can't continue in a civilization based on unbridled materialism, greed, and violence.

This is a time for reflection. What kind of world do we want? I think this is the most important question of our time, the question that every woman and every man with awareness should ask, the question the caliph of Baghdad should have asked the thief in the old tale.

We want a world of beauty, not only that which the senses appreciate, but also the beauty perceived by an open heart and a clear mind. We want a pristine planet protected from all forms of aggression. We want a balanced and sustainable civilization based on mutual respect, and respect for other species and for nature. We want an inclusive and egalitarian civilization free of gender, race, class, and age discrimination, and any other classification that separates us. We want the kind of world where peace, empathy, decency, truth, and compassion prevail. Above all, we want a joyful world. That is what we, the good witches, want. It's not a fantasy, it's a project. Together we can achieve it.

When the coronavirus crisis is over we will crawl from our lairs and cautiously enter a new normal, and the first thing we will do is hug one another in the streets. How we have missed touching people! We will cherish each encounter and tend kindly to the matters of the heart.

ACKNOWLEDGMENTS

I am truly grateful to:

Lori Barra and Sarah Hillesheim for the wonderful work they do at our foundation.

Johanna Castillo, Lluís Palomares, and Maribel Luque, my agents, who came up with the idea of writing about feminism.

Jennifer Hershey, Nuria Tey, and David Trías, my editors at Ballantine and Plaza & Janés.

Kavita Ramdas for being a mentor at my foundation and sharing with me her knowledge about women's issues worldwide.

Laura Palomares for her insights about young feminists.

Lauren Cuthbert for editing my translation into English.

The heroines I meet every day through my foundation, who shared their stories with me and inspired this book.

The feminists who shaped me as a young woman and still guide my life.

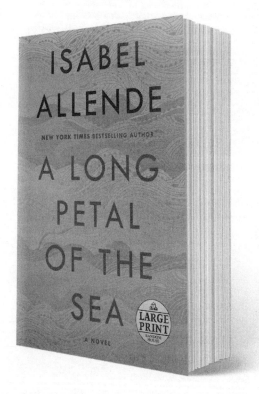